THE ULTIMATE Rubber Stamping
TECHNIQUE BOOK

Gail Green

Published by

KRAUSE PUBLICATIONS

700 East State St., Iola, WI 54990-0001
Telephone (715) 445-2214
www.krause.com

Please call or write for our free catalog of publications. Our toll-free number to place an order or obtain a free catalog is 800-258-0929 or please use our regular business telephone 715-445-2214 for editorial comment and further information.

Library of Congress Catalog Number 98-87379
ISBN 0-87341-703-8

The following registered trademark terms and companies appear in this publication:

Pop Dots™ (All Night Media, Inc.); Patio Paint™ (DecoArt); Aleene's® Premium-Coat™ acrylic paints, varnishes, and mediums and Tulip® Fabric Paint (Duncan Enterprises); The Masters® Brush Cleaner and Kimberly® Water Color Pencils (General Pencil Co.); "Craftwares™" pre-sewn products (Janlynn Corporation); Leather Stampables™ leather products (The Leather Factory); Stamp Décor™, Decorator Blocks®, Mod Podge®, Decorator Glazes, Folk Art® acrylic paints, varnishes, and painting mediums (Plaid Enterprises, Inc.); Decorative™ Foam Stamps (Rubber Stampede); Iron-on HeatnBond® and pressure-sensitive PeelnStick™ and Keep a Memory™ adhesives and laminates (Therm O Web, Inc.); Dual Brush-Pen Markers, Mono® Adhesive and Liquid Glue (Tombow); Encore!™ Ultimate Metallic Pigment Ink, Fabrico™ Premium Multi-Purpose Craft Ink and Dual Markers, Emboss Dual Pen and Embossing Stamp Pad, Kaleidacolor™, and Impress™ Dye Inkpads (Tsukineko®, Inc.)

All stamp images used with permission ©1999 from the following:

All Night Media, Inc., Good Stamps Stamp Goods, Hero Arts Rubber Stamps, Inc., Maine Street Stamps, Marks of Distinction, Plaid Enterprises, Inc., Red Hot Rubber!, Inc., Rubber Stampede, and Stampendous, Inc.

Foreword

Rubber stamping enthusiasts... this is the book you've been waiting for! Whether you've just experienced the joy of creating your first rubber stamp design or you've long been addicted to the pleasure of rubber stamping, Gail Green is here to take you on a creative adventure.

Gail's enthusiastic approach and thorough instructions will quickly take you through mastering the basic techniques of rubber stamping. Then it's on to endless creative possibilities as she explores a wide variety of techniques that will stimulate even experienced stampers. Her goof-proof techniques and clear step-by-step instructions and photos will guide you through challenging projects with confidence. It is easy to get caught up in Gail's passion for exploring rubber stamping in new and exciting ways as she introduces fresh approaches to conventional methods and expands on basic techniques and materials.

You will find yourself returning to *The Ultimate Rubber Stamping Technique Book* again and again as you use it as a valuable resource for basic information and a constant source of inspiration.

Julie Stephani
Great American Crafts magazine Editor

Dedication

This book is dedicated to my family—Jeff, Jason, and Katie—for enduring endless piles of works in progress, fellow designer and friend, Deb Parks, for her support and words of encouragement, all of the many wonderful people in the creative craft industry who have generously assisted with the projects, supplied information and materials, photography, and editorial assistance, but most of all, to the Master who has blessed the work of my hands.

A special word of thanks to the following for their dedication to this project:
Editorial: Amy Tincher-Durik
Book design: Jan Wojtech
Step-by-step photography: Thomas Manning
Additional photography: Ross Hubbard and Kris Kandler
Models: Katie Green, Penni Jess, Liliya Dzhorayeva, and Joey Hirsh

In loving memory of Madison, my quintessential Border Collie, who thought of yet another creative use for rubber stamps...

Table of Contents

Note: All projects designed by Gail Green, except those on pages 28, 38, 39, 49, 60, 85, 111, and 120 (Deb Parks); page 113 (Kari Lee) for The Leather Factory; page 52 (Barbara Barnes); and page 100 (Karen Johnson) for All Night Media, Inc.

Introduction

Rubber stamping is an adventure. It is a wonderful, magical odyssey into a creative realm that is continually unfolding—and where new ideas are always waiting to be explored.

We all grew up with rubber stamps, but we just never thought of them as being fun. Remember that disappointing envelope with "Return to Sender" stamped on it with the ominous pointing finger, or all of the various business stamps used in offices and libraries around the globe? All rather boring stuff.

But, not so long ago (sometime in the mid-1970s), in a land not so far away (somewhere on the West Coast), rubber stamps were gradually transformed into rubber *art* stamps and *that* sparked a whole new creative phenomenon! Growing at first in California, and then spreading slowly to a few other parts of the country, rubber stamping began to make its mark—literally. Although these new artistic stamps were first used to create mail art (like postcards with hand-stamped scenes and messages), people soon began creating everything from their own unique greeting cards and gift wraps to invitations and bookmarks.

When the creative craft industry adopted rubber stamping as a new craft trend in the mid-1990s, artistic stamping gained even more momentum. New and creative ways of using stamps were discovered and explored. This medium seemed to be so versatile that it could be used to decorate almost *any* solid surface! In fact, because rubber stamps *can* be used on so many surfaces and in so many different ways, they have kept pace with almost every crafting trend. With the continual introduction of new stamping ideas, techniques, and products, coupled with the enthusiasm of thousands of totally devoted stampers, there seems to be no end in sight to the creative potentials of rubber stamping.

Rubber stamping spans generations, sexes, and cultural differences. Anyone who can hold a rubber stamp in his or her hand and make contact on paper can learn to stamp! I met my first rubber stamp 10 years ago and fell madly, deeply, passionately in love. Stamping is one of the most creative mediums I have ever worked in. Simply put, rubber stamping is great fun! And the more stamping I do, the more I discover how much more I can do with these stamps. As my stamping knowledge and skills have grown over the years, so have my enthusiasm and eagerness to continue exploring new ways to create with rubber stamps.

This creative medium appeals to both artists and the artistically-challenged alike. Rubber stamps can turn anyone into an instant artist. If you have difficulty drawing a straight line, stamping beautifully-drawn images onto a project can become intoxicating!

There is some dispute as to whether rubber stamping should be considered an art form or merely a crafting medium. Some argue that the mechanics of stamping merely serve to reproduce images that are already pre-drawn and, because these images are just copies of another artist's inspiration, any items created through stamping are not really pieces of art. Yet others, including myself, feel that it is *because* of these pre-drawn images that we are freed from the tedious hand drafting of individual images to more fully explore and create pieces of art based on a number of multiple techniques and learned skills.

So, would a real artist be caught with a stamp in his or her hand? You bet! Like hundreds of other rubber stamp artists, I've been drawing since I was old enough to hold a crayon and scribble on walls. A professional illustrator for years, I have drawn hundreds of images from concept to finished line art. Rubber stamps, however, have given me the freedom to explore and design in the same way the computer has freed up graphic artists across the globe. All of us are probably aware that there is actually a lot more involved in creating a work of art than just drawing. Had Michelangelo,

Rembrandt, or Picasso not developed such a heightened sense of design, composition, and color, their masterpieces would not have had the same impact. Many of the techniques involved in rubber stamping actually help teach—and reinforce—those very important skills by removing the need to do the hand drafting of each individual image. Rubber stamps place the possibility of having the same image repeated over and over again on a sheet of paper, in a matter of seconds, at our disposal. Manipulating images on a computer takes more time than that! I believe that rubber stamping is no less an art form than high-tech pieces generated through computer manipulation. And, try as I might—even with a hundred lifetimes—I would never have enough time (or be able) to draw all of the thousands of wonderful images in all of the subjects and styles available in rubber stamp form. Rubber stamps allow each of us to accomplish so much in so little time!

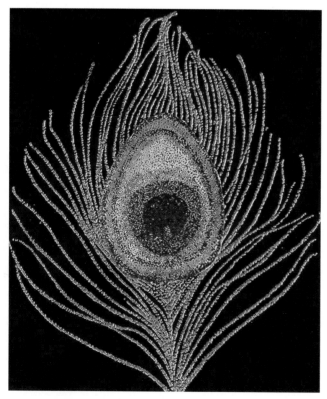

Rubber stamping brings instant gratification to those of us with limited free time. Most people can achieve very satisfying results with minimal time and effort. Many projects in this book can be completed in just a few minutes, with results that defy their ease. Plus, unlike many other crafts that require elaborate work space, rubber stamping can be done at a kitchen table or desk. Basic techniques can be learned quite quickly, and even the more advanced skills are surprisingly easy to master.

With the world becoming increasingly immersed with so many sterile, non-tactile technologies, stamping simply feels good to do. There is something very therapeutic about the physical act of pressing a stamp into an ink pad and then again onto paper. I have seen that unmistakable look of pure joy on children's faces when they stamp their first images. It is magic! Stamping can return each of us to a gentler time, where pleasures were simple and satisfaction laid in the work of your hands.

The Ultimate Rubber Stamping Technique Book is your complete guide to the fascinating world of rubber stamps. From tips and techniques to project demonstrations, all of the information you could possibly need to become a successful stamper is right here! So, whether you are an experienced stamper or are just beginning your journey, you will soon discover that the creative possibilities are endless.

Now, grab your stamps and let the adventure begin!

Chapter 1

Meet Your Materials

The key for unlocking the magic of rubber stamping is simple: learn the basics! The first thing you need to do is meet your materials.

Left: Rubber stamps come in a wide variety of sizes, styles, and shapes. Some even have foam or sponge-like materials, instead of rubber, to create the image portion of the stamp.

Below: Close-up of a scored foam-mounted rubber stamp set.

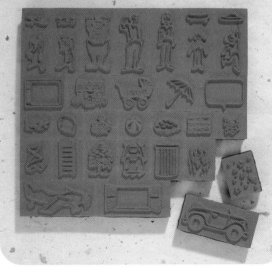

RUBBER STAMPS

Rubber stamps are certainly not difficult to find. They can be purchased at gift, craft, toy, and rubber stamp specialty stores, through mail order catalogs, at various rubber stamp conventions held throughout the country (and overseas), over the Internet, and through home parties.

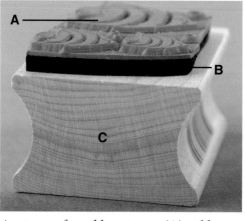

Anatomy of a rubber stamp: (A) rubber die, (B) foam cushion, and (C) wood mount

From holiday, ethnic, and Victorian themes to animals, people, and cartoons, there are certainly enough variety of images available to appeal to everyone's tastes! Rubber stamp images run the gamut from the cute and whimsical to the totally weird and grotesque—and there are dozens of other categories in between.

Most rubber stamps consist of a **rubber die** (which contains the image), a **foam cushion**, and a **mount** or handle (which can be either wood, foam, or plastic).

The rubber can contain either a solid or an outline image and can be with or without detail. An **outline image**

A color index

rubber stamp consists of a line drawing that can be colored in, while a **solid image** stamp has an image that is completely or almost completely filled in. Choose rubber stamps that have clean, deep etching—they make the best imprints.

The foam cushion is a thin piece of foam that is positioned between the rubber die and the mount. One of its functions is to raise the rubber higher off of the mount. This helps ensure that the only portion of the stamp that will get ink on it when pressed into an ink pad is the rubber. The foam cushion also distributes pressure more evenly to give a stamp better performance and stability.

Wood-mounted rubber stamps contain an image of the stamp, called an **index**, which is printed on the top of the wood mount. The indexing can be either a simple black and white line drawing, which is an exact reproduction of the stamp image, or a color drawing. Color indexing grabs the eye and offers the consumer a glimpse into the possibilities of the particular image. Keep in mind, however, that color indexing is merely a suggestion of how a stamped image might look when various coloring methods are used. The initial stamped image will still be a single color line drawing or solid image.

Foam-mounted stamps are typically less expensive than wood-mounted versions and usually come in sets of multiple images. There are also clear plastic-mounted stamps available that make positioning images easier. Novelty stamps even come on rollers, on the end of a pencil, or as part of a toy! Large, solid-image home decorating and fabric stamps may contain a single or multi-sectioned sponge or foam image attached to a heavy foam mount. There are even stamps that consist solely of a single, scored, cut-out foam or sponge shape with no mount at all.

THE MAKING OF A RUBBER STAMP

All rubber stamps begin with an illustration, whether it is hand-drawn in pen and ink or computer-manipulated. Regardless, the artist must take great care in preparing the drawing properly so it will imprint clearly as a stamp. After the finished size has been determined, multiple copies of camera-ready art are made and placed in a grid-like pattern, from which a transparency is created. This "negative" is then used to create a raised image metal plate on a medium such as magnesium (known as a mag plate). Magnesium plates result in very detailed, deeply-etched images. A mold is then made from matrix board (a special, dry, heavily-condensed moldable paper). This mold, along with a blank sheet of rubber, is placed into a machine called a vulcanizer. Rubber needs to be cured with heat and pressure to flow properly into the mold, with as little waste as possible. Pressed against the matrix board and heated at temperatures ranging from 325° to 500°F (depending on the amount of time determined for curing), the rubber softens and molds into the images on the plate. When cool, the impressed rubber is attached to the foam cushion, cut out, and secured to a wood mount.

The actual wood mount and the assembly of wood-mounted stamps adds to the cost of these stamps. A good, economical alternative are foam-mounted stamp sets which contain multiple coordinating images. These sets are not hand-trimmed; they are die-cut with special machines. Because they are not trimmed close to the image, however, the edge of the stamp can leave a "back-print" on your projects. (A "back-print" is the transfer of ink onto your project surface from an area of the stamp other than the actual image.) To avoid this unwanted effect, trim the excess foam away with a sharp, small-pointed scissors and mount the stamps onto wood with a permanent adhesive.

TIP: IF THE RUBBER COMES OFF OF ITS FOAM OR WOOD MOUNT, RE-ATTACH IT WITH PERMANENT ADHESIVE.

INK

There are many different types and brands of inks that can be used for rubber stamping. Ink pads are made with either a recessed or raised pad on top of a plastic base. The advantage of a raised pad is that it can accommodate large stamps. Most ink is available in solid colors or in rainbow color combinations. The two most commonly used inks are dye and pigment.

Dye ink is water-based and comes in both a washable child-safe version and a more permanent type. It penetrates into and stains the fibers beneath the surface being stamped on. This ink dries quickly, making it perfect for children and fast, easy projects. Dye inks give very crisp images, especially when stamped on glossy, coated papers. The two drawbacks to dye ink are that the color tends to fade with time or exposure to light and it tends to stain the stamp's rubber. Dye inks come in recessed or raised pads and are available in either solid or rainbow colors. Through time and use, the different colored sections in the rainbow dye ink pad will bleed together.

Pigment ink is more permanent than dye ink and dries slowly because it adheres to the stamping surface rather than soaking into it. This ink comes in a wide range of colors, including attractive rainbow and palette combination pads. Pigment ink will dry quickly when sprinkled with embossing powder and heated in a process called thermography (more commonly known as embossing). However, because these inks take so long to dry when not embossed, they are unsuitable for children, coated non-porous surfaces, and projects that need to dry quickly.

Embossing ink and **fabric ink** are also used for rubber stamping. Although they are covered more extensively in Chapters 7 and 9, respectively, here are some general notes.

Examples of dye-based ink pads, including a rainbow pad (left) and assorted solid color raised pads

An assortment of non-toxic fabric ink pads

Embossing ink is clear or lightly-tinted pigment ink that is used with opaque embossing powders. It dries very slowly. Because it is transparent, embossing ink is easy to clean off a stamp's surface.

Fabric inks are available in several different brands. Some fabric inks (and their cleaners) are solvent-based and, therefore, contain irritants or are toxic. Check labels carefully and use caution when using these types of inks. Other fabric inks are pigment-based, non-toxic, and safer to use, but require an extra step called heat setting (see page 103) to completely retain their permanence on fabric. Because most fabric inks are very permanent on fabric, make sure to protect your clothing and work surface when using them.

> NOTE: SOME INK MANUFACTURERS OFFER REFILL BOTTLES OF INK, CALLED "RE-INKERS." A DRIED INK PAD CAN QUICKLY BE RESTORED WITH A FEW DROPS OF INK FROM ONE OF THESE BOTTLES.

Embossing supplies. Clockwise around the central multi-colored pigment ink pad, beginning at left center: tinted clear embossing ink pad, opaque embossing powders, silver metallic pigment ink pad, small pigment ink cubes, sparkle embossing powder, two-sided "Dauber Duos" (Tsukineko), and gold metallic pigment ink pad

PAINTS AND GLAZES

Stamping paint, as well as translucent glazes and specially-formulated outdoor paints, are relatively new additions to the stamping repertoire. Acrylic paints (mixed with special mediums) and fabric paints can also be used with bolder or more solid-type stamp images, but you will get the best results if you use paints or glazes that are formulated for use with rubber stamps. Because these paints can dry very quickly and ruin your stamp, however, extra care must be taken to wash the paint off of your stamp immediately after use or several times during a lengthy stamping session. If this is not possible, keep the painted image side of the stamp on a damp paper towel to prevent the paint from drying completely until it can be cleaned. Most of these paints and glazes can be used on walls and wood, as well as leather and fabric, because they are permanent and fade-resistant. Make sure to follow the manufacturer's instructions for each specific product.

An example of stamping glaze

EMBOSSING POWDERS

Embossing literally offers a new dimension in stamping. When embossing powders are sprinkled onto a stamped image and heated properly, the embossing powder melts and raises off of the surface to create a 3-D effect. Embossing, especially in gold or silver, can add quite an elegant touch to any project. The solid embossed outline also acts as a resist, making it easier to color the stamped image.

Used with slow-drying embossing or pigment inks, embossing powders come in a variety of colors and tints. Powder colors range from opaque metallics and colors that echo pigment ink pad colors to bright neon colors and soft pastels.

Two commonly used embossing powders are opaque and clear. Opaque embossing powders can be used over clear embossing ink or over any of the pigment ink in colors that fall within the same color range. Clear embossing powders must be used over colored ink. These transparent powders were designed to allow the color of the ink to show through. The clear powders are ideal to use with rainbow ink pads or to create other multiple color images. Some clear embossing powders (as well as some opaque powders) have a bit of finely-ground glitter in them which gives an image a little sparkle.

Some of the more unusual embossing powders include the slightly translucent pearl powders and faux finish mixtures. The pearl powders have a hint of color and will tint the ink in which the image is stamped. Pearls are fun to test on different ink colors; the interesting color effects can be quite surprising. And, faux finish mixtures, such as verdigris or enamelware, can make a stamped image look as exotic as their names!

HEAT TOOLS

Embossing guns are the easiest heating tool to use when embossing, because they provide the most even heat temperature, and you can more easily control the exact area you

Heat tool used for embossing

wish to heat, but use with caution! The tip of the standard embossing gun reaches temperatures hot enough to melt paint! This metal tip will remain very hot for up to 15 minutes after use. For safety, always position the tip away from you when returning the gun to the table or holder after using. Some heat guns now come with safety tips or use a lower temperature.

Other possible heating methods include the following: holding the stamped image a few inches above a traditional toaster, or a few inches away from a non-steam set iron, or near a light bulb. It can be more difficult to control your results, however, using these methods.

WARNING: NEVER PLACE A PROJECT INSIDE OF A TOASTER OR TOASTER OVEN OR TOUCH A PROJECT DIRECTLY WITH A HEATED IRON!

COLORING TOOLS

There are many fine-tip, calligraphy, and watercolor brush markers available to add the excitement of color to your stamped image. Better-quality markers are specially suited to blend and shade, making it possible to obtain professional results with very little effort. The dazzling color palettes and "blendability" make markers ideal for most paper projects.

Besides these markers, you can also use embossing markers and colored pencils, or try sponging color onto a stamped image. Embossing markers contain a special slower-drying ink which will hold embossing powder long enough to be heated and melted. These pens dry faster than pigment or embossing ink, so you need to work quickly and complete small sections at a time. If you prefer a softer, more muted color palette, though, try colored pencils.

Colored pencils, which are easy to use, can be applied on any non-glossy paper. Another fun method of coloring in your stamped images is by sponging color onto the paper using ink from your stamp pad. Sponging some color around a template can also add an interesting background statement.

For more information on all of these and other coloring tools and techniques, see Chapter 4.

OTHER SUPPLIES

There are several other products currently on the market which are commonly used in conjunction with rubber stamping. Some of these items are

Embellishment tools, top row (from left to right): crimping tool, stamp positioner, decorative-edge scissors, pre-cut double-sided adhesive foam tape; bottom row (from left to right): stamping sponges, hard rubber brayer, sponge brayer, decorative shape punch, liquid glue (two), solid glue stick, glitter glue, metallic confetti shapes, fine-textured glitter

considered stamping aids, while others serve to enhance the stamped images themselves. Primarily embellishment tools, these items are thought of as basic equipment to stamping aficionados.

• **Punches** can come in an assortment of designs and shapes that will punch out shapes called confetti. These are then glued onto stamped creations.

• **Glitter** is a favorite among many, especially in the younger arena. Unlike metallic school glitters, however, these finely-ground glitters are easy to clean up. They come in a dazzling array of colors and add a special sparkle to many projects.

• **Glitter glue** is colored translucent glue that has glitter mixed with it. It dries slowly and is usually used for projects that have more time to dry.

• **Glues and adhesives** can be used with your rubber-stamped projects. These include glue pens, glue sticks, roll-on or press-on adhesives, liquid glues and adhesives, mounting tapes, laminates, and iron-on adhesives. Some are available as either permanent or temporary bond.

• A **crimping tool** resembles a device used to wring tubes of paint or toothpaste. This product, however, has a pattern on the rubber roller that gives paper a crimped texture.

• A **stamp positioner** is a T- or L-shaped tool designed to accurately align images. (See page 32 for correct use.)

For hard-to-clean metallic ink or paint that was left to dry, The Masters Brush Cleaner and Preserver (General Pencil) does wonders on rubber, as well as dirty brushes (left and center). Keep your stamps clean by dabbing specially-formulated stamp cleaner onto the inked rubber and wiping off the dissolved ink (right).

Other essential supplies every stamper needs include:
• Sharp, small-tipped scissors
• Ruler (preferably metal, with a cork bottom)
• Rags
• Proper lighting (an evenly well-lit area without many cast shadows)
• Clean, flat stamping surface (protected with a clean, smooth paper cover, such as a large sheet of newsprint)
• Scrap paper
• Containers to help organize your supplies

CARE OF SUPPLIES

Rubber stamps need to be cleaned each time you change ink type or color and before they are put away. It is easier to clean most inks off if you clean your stamps after each stamping session. Rubber stamps should never be submerged in liquid of any kind! The rubber surface can be cleaned with a specially-formulated stamp cleaner or alcohol-free baby wipes. Stamp cleaner is applied directly to inked rubber with a dabbing motion. A textured rag or terry cloth towel is then used to wipe the dissolved ink away. Blotting the rubber onto a damp towel should be adequate for washable, child-safe ink. Paints and glazes might require a little more rubbing. For stubborn dried-on ink or paint, non-toxic "The Masters" Brush Cleaner and Preserver will work wonders (a lifesaver for stamping sponges and paint brushes, too!).

With a little bit of care, rubber stamps can last a lifetime and give many hours of pleasure to every hand that holds them.

MORE TIPS:

• STORE YOUR STAMPS AWAY FROM DIRECT HEAT OR SUNLIGHT TO PREVENT THE RUBBER FROM DETERIORATING OR TURNING BRITTLE.

• OLD TERRY CLOTH TOWELS CONTAIN AN ABRASIVE SURFACE THAT CAN HELP REMOVE PAINT AND GLAZE FROM RUBBER OR FOAM STAMPS.

• A SMALL TOOTHBRUSH CAN HELP SCRUB AWAY STUBBORN BITS OF DRIED INK.

Chapter 2
Basic Stamping Techniques 101

These projects use only basic stamping techniques.

One of the most important keys to successful stamping is practice, practice, practice! Your mom was right—the more you do something, the better you get! Always practice your impression a few times on scrap paper before beginning your actual project. This will help you get familiar with the individuality of the stamp(s) you have chosen to work with. There is nothing more frustrating than nearing completion on a fantastic-looking project and, then, making a poor imprint with an untried stamp!

Dress up a gift quickly with easy-to-stamp wrapping paper and a matching note card.

You might discover that pressure may need to be applied a little differently with each stamp you are using. Outline images stamp differently than the more solid images most commonly used for fabric and home decor stamping. One stamp may need more pressure in the center so the image prints more solidly, while another might need more or less pressure on an edge or detail to print clearly. Also, stamping on a vertical or three-dimensional surface, such as a wall or a box, feels very different from stamping on a horizontal surface. Before attempting to decorate different types of untextured surfaces, make sure you practice stamping on one first!

Surface textures can also affect your image quality. One stamp may give great results on a smooth-surfaced paper, but may be disappointing when stamped on an expensive piece of textured, handmade paper. Make sure to practice stamping first on similar textures, using the same ink or paint you will be using for the actual project.

The extra few minutes this important step might take will pay off in the end! Plus, this "practice" habit will become even more valuable when you try your hand on surfaces such as fabric, wood, or leather. The ink and paint used on fabric and leather are quite permanent, so there is no margin for error with these materials. Mistakes with permanent ink and paint cannot be erased or completely washed out. Also, when you begin creating projects with complex patterns or positioning, work the "bugs" out on scrap paper first. Solving spacing or positioning questions on something that "doesn't count" takes the pressure off!

If this all sounds rather intimidating, be assured that rubber stamping is one of the easiest and most enjoyable art forms to learn! Its unprecedented growth in the past several years will attest to that, as will the thousands of stamping enthusiasts. The instructions in the following chapters will give you all of the guidance you need to become a successful stamper.

But first, some basic pointers:
● Always protect your work surface while stamping with a simple protective covering, such as paper.
● Make sure your work surface is smooth, hard, and flat.
● Clean stamps make clean imprints! Always check the rubber image area before stamping to clean off forgotten ink, glitter specks, or paper scraps. Check your ink pad for debris, too!
● Always practice your imprint on scrap paper before stamping on your finished project.
● Trim excess rubber from non-image areas of the stamp that are producing a back-print.
● Test your ink pad to see if it has dried out. If necessary, re-ink the pad or use a new one.
● Work in an area that is out of direct sunlight or wind. Both will dry out your ink pad and affect embossing results. A bright, evenly-lit work area that is indoors is best.
● Always clean your stamp before changing ink colors!
● As with other art materials, wear suitable clothing while stamping, making sure that sleeves are elbow height or above. Always wear a smock to protect good clothing.

Now, let's get started! Follow these simple, step-by-step instructions for stamping success!

HOW TO STAMP

Pressing an inked stamp onto paper requires even pressure over the entire stamp surface to ensure a complete, clear image. When stamping with a large, over-sized stamp, hold the stamp firmly and carefully in place with one hand, while applying pressure over the entire wood mount with the other. By moving your pressing hand from spot to spot on the mount, the entire image area—especially the center—will receive even pressure. You can also use a block of wood to press with. (Hint: Use a second wood-mounted stamp that has been placed rubber side up for your pressing block.)

Pressing a stamp into a dye ink pad feels different than pressing it into a pigment or fabric pad. The pad surface on a dye ink pad is hard and requires a firm touch. Because of this, you will need to apply more pressure when tapping your stamp on this pad. Conversely, pigment and fabric ink pads require a gentler pressure. If you press your stamp too hard into these pads, your stamp will literally "sink" into the pad, transferring unwanted ink onto the rubber trim and wood mount.

To stamp, you'll need:
    Dye ink pad   Rubber stamp
    Piece of paper

1. Tap the stamp on an ink pad until the entire image area is evenly inked.

2. Using even pressure, press the stamp down firmly onto a piece of paper. Try to avoid rocking the stamp or pressing extremely hard because these movements will blur the image.

3. Lift the stamp straight off of the paper. Allow the ink to dry.

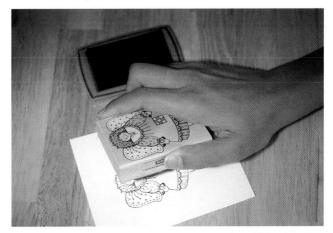

TIP: IT IS BEST TO USE BOTH HANDS WHEN STAMPING WITH A LARGE-SIZED STAMP. PLACE THE INKED STAMP ONTO THE PAPER, HOLD THE STAMP IN PLACE WITH ONE HAND, AND USE YOUR OTHER HAND TO PRESS EVENLY ALL AROUND THE ENTIRE STAMP.

HOW TO EMBOSS

Heating and melting embossing powder that has been sprinkled over slow-drying pigment ink reduces the ink's drying time to a matter of seconds! The recommended way to emboss is to heat from underneath the paper's surface, allowing the paper to heat and evenly melt the powder. It is easier, however, to heat from above with the heat gun until you feel more comfortable with the embossing process. That way, you can more easily judge the distance the heat source is from the paper surface. Remember that you need to use only opaque embossing powder with embossing ink, but you can use either clear or opaque powder over colored pigment ink.

To emboss, you'll need:
    Pigment ink pad
    Clear embossing powder
    Piece of paper
    Heat tool
    Sheet of scrap paper
    Fine, dry paintbrush

NOTE: YOU MAY ALSO EMBOSS USING CLEAR OR TINTED EMBOSSING INK AND OPAQUE EMBOSSING POWDER

1. First, follow the steps above (How to Stamp) to stamp an image. Then, sprinkle embossing powder over the entire image.

2. Tap off the excess powder onto a sheet of scrap paper or directly into the container. If a bit of the powder clings to your paper outside of the image area, gently brush it off with a very fine, dry paintbrush.

3. Heat the image evenly with an embossing tool until the powder melts. **Do not overheat or the powder will scorch!** The best way to tell if the powder is melting is to view the image at a slight angle while it is being heated; the powder begins to "dance" right before it melts and will start to change color slightly. Remove the heat source as soon as the

entire image has changed color. Let the embossed image cool for a few seconds before touching it.

REPEAT DESIGN

This is the most fundamental—and essential—technique to use with rubber stamps. This is the first stamping discovery that makes individual stamps come alive! There are two basic types of repeats:

1. Patterned repeat: Stamp one (or more) image(s) over and over in a specific pattern. This can be accomplished by repeating a single image or by using alternating multiple images in rows or other patterned groupings. This technique adds symmetry and balance to a project.

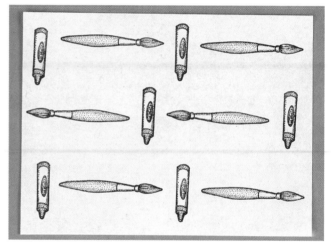

2. Random repeat: Stamp one (or more) image(s) repeatedly without any pattern. Repeating single or multiples images in a non-patterned manner creates an asymmetrical design feature which can add interest to projects that seem a bit static.

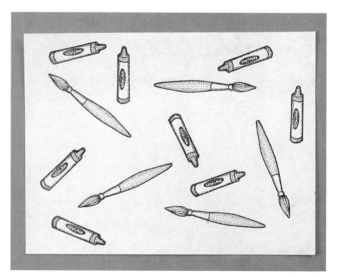

Repeat design techniques allow you to make patterns, backgrounds, borders, and frames. Use color in addition to your image repetition to reinforce the patterns you create. Stamp along the edges of your project to create borders or frames. Use a single or specially-designed border stamp in a repeat pattern. Large background stamps are designed for repeating to create quick, interesting backgrounds and textures.

MASKING

Masking creates the illusion of depth through over-lapping images. This trick is accomplished by placing a separate cut-out of an image (referred to as a "mask") over the same image which has already been stamped on your project. The same image is then stamped again, overlapping it slightly onto the mask. **Always begin with the image you will want to appear in front first!**

Masking works best with mid- to large-sized stamps that have a definite outlined stamp image. (Small stamp images may be difficult to mask, because it can be hard to cover small images easily.)

To mask, you'll need:
  Rubber stamp (with a definite outlined
    stamp image)
  Dye ink pad (different colored pads were
    used for this demonstration)
  Piece of paper
  Scissors
  Scrap paper or Post-it note

1. Stamp your image on a piece of scrap paper or a Post-it note. Carefully cut the image out on the image side of the outline. Make sure you cut just within the outline so that it is slightly smaller than the stamped image. This will be your mask.

2. Stamp your front image first on your project surface. Let the ink dry or complete the embossing process if you are embossing your images.

3. Cover this first image with your mask. Holding the mask in place, stamp your second image, slightly overlapping onto the masked area.

4. Lift your stamp off and carefully remove the mask. Your first image should look as if it is in front of the second image.

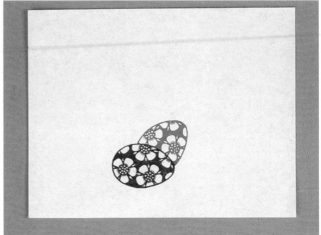

Each time the image you wish to cover changes, you will need to create a new matching mask shape. You will also need to create duplicate masks when an image you want to stamp will appear staggered behind two images. Then you will have to hold **both** masks in place as you stamp the new image.

MULTIPLE IMAGE MASKING

While executing this technique, keep in mind that unless you are creating an unusual perspective, such as a bird's eye view, the object(s) closest to the viewer should be positioned lower down on the paper. As you mask and stamp images, the objects receding into the distance should be positioned progressively higher on the page. This simple technique will add a dimension of realism to your projects, especially when creating multiple image scenes.

To create a multiple-image mask, you'll need:
   Two or more rubber stamps (here, eggs and a bunny were used)
   Dye ink pad (different colored pads were used for this demonstration)
   Piece of paper
   Scissors
   Scrap paper or Post-It note

1. Stamp the same egg twice, masking as before.

2. Place a single bunny in the middle of all of the eggs by stamping a bunny image behind one of the eggs.

3. In order to stamp more eggs behind the bunny, you will now need to stamp and cut out a bunny mask to place over the single bunny image.

With multiple image masking, objects appear to be in front or behind each other. This gives your scene a more realistic appearance.

Chapter 3

And Now... More Stamping Techniques

Now that you feel comfortable with basic stamping techniques, it's time to move on to some of the more challenging concepts.

These stamped note cards and wrapping paper are examples of stamping off the edge.

STAMPING OFF THE EDGE

This versatile technique allows you to use stamp images that extend beyond the edges of your project. Stamping off the edge provides an easy way to continue a repeat pattern regardless of the project's physical dimensions. This process also creates a seamless look when stamping on projects, such as wrapping paper or note cards, where it is desirable for the entire space to be filled with repeated stamp images.

Stamping off the edge also makes it possible to continue a design or pattern around an outside square corner of a three-dimensional project, such as a box or tray. Even if only a portion of an image has been stamped on one flat side of an object, the remainder of the image can easily be imprinted around the corner onto the adjoining surface by following these easy steps as outlined in this demonstration.

NOTE: UNLESS OTHERWISE LISTED, ALL OF THE TECHNIQUES DESCRIBED IN THIS CHAPTER REQUIRE RUBBER STAMPS, DYE INK PADS, PAPER OR CARD STOCK, SCRAP PAPER, AND SCISSORS (STRAIGHT-EDGE OR DECORATIVE).

STAMPING OFF THE EDGE ON A 3-D SURFACE (PAPIER MÂCHÉ BOX)

MATERIALS

Small outline fish and bubble rubber stamps*
Black dye ink pad
Light blue acrylic paint
Papier mâché box
Paintbrush

Used in this project: *#489D Fish Lips (All Night Media) and #LL252 Sea Life Set (Hero Arts Rubber Stamps)

1. Paint the lid and box separately with acrylic paint. Let both pieces dry completely.

2. Position your inked stamp so it extends over one corner edge of the box. Press in place and then lift the stamp slightly off of the surface.

3. Change the angle of your hand to position the remainder of the stamp image around the corner, over the adjoining surface. Again, the stamp should extend over the edge. Without reapplying ink, press the stamp in place, stamping only the remaining unstamped portion of the image.

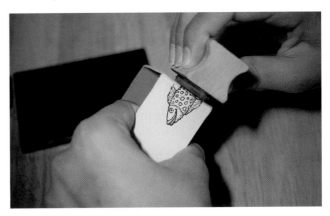

4. Continue stamping your pattern on that side of the box. Repeat Steps 1 and 2 when you get to the next edge. Continue in this manner until the box is complete. Stamp the lid, stamping off the edge as well, if desired.

NON-IMAGE MASKING

Non-image masking can also supply an "artificial" edge to stamp an image off of. Stamping onto a straight edge "mask" offers you the flexibility to use portions of stamp images to create unusual effects. By doing so, you have essentially simulated an edge, enabling you to stamp only a portion of your image.

By placing a straight edge "mask" (a square piece of paper) onto these two cards, I was able to stamp only a portion of the stamps each time. The parts of the images I wanted to print on the card did, and the remaining parts imprinted on the mask instead. First, for the card on the left, I stamped the upper portion of the dog, masking off the bottom portion of the image. Next, I placed the mask over the stamped image of the dog's head and stamped only the bottom portion of the cat's body. Practice on scrap paper first when matching two different images such as the dog and cat or the ice cream cone and fish. The birthday card on the right has a simple repeat across the top and bottom edges, using the candle portion only of the Happy Birthday stamp shown. I achieved this look by masking off the words each time I stamped the image across the top row and by stamping off the bottom edge on the bottom row.

> **TIP:** ALWAYS STAMP OFF THE EDGE ONTO AN EXTRA PIECE OF SCRAP PAPER WHEN DOING TWO-DIMENSIONAL PROJECTS SUCH AS THESE.

STAMPING ON A CURVED SURFACE (PAPIER MÂCHÉ BOX)

STAMPING ON A CURVED SURFACE

Most of the surfaces you will stamp on are flat, but you can learn to stamp on a curved surface, such as a terra cotta pot or oval container, by following these easy steps as outlined in this demonstration.

MATERIALS

Small outline sun and solid star rubber stamps*
Yellow and country blue dye ink pads
LIght tan and royal blue acrylic paint
Round or oval papier mâché box
Paintbrush

Used in this project: *#525A Star (All Night Media, Inc.);
#F253 Serene Sun (Hero Arts Rubber Stamps, Inc.)

1. Paint the lid and box separately with acrylic paint. Let both pieces dry completely.

2. Press an inked stamp onto your curved surface so that the center of the stamp makes firm contact with the box's surface.

3. Without lifting or moving the stamp, maintain an even pressure and roll the stamp to the left.

4. Roll the stamp back to the center point and then to the right, exerting even pressure the entire time.

5. Remove the stamp by lifting it straight off of the surface.

6. Repeat Steps 2 to 5 until the box is complete. Stamp the lid as desired.

CUT EDGES

There are three basic techniques available for creating decorated cut edges: simple cut edges, stamped cut-outs, and cut-edge layers. To create these looks, you will need either straight-edge or decorative-edge scissors, as specified.

SIMPLE CUT EDGES

1. Cut along the open edge(s) of the note card using a pair of specially-designed decorative-edge scissors.

2. To emphasize any of the decorative edges you have cut, use color techniques, such as sponging (see page 41), a coordinating stamp pattern, or embellishments like ribbon or glitter on the inside edge that is now exposed.

STAMPED CUT-OUTS

1. Stamp an image repeatedly along the straight front edge of a note card. Make sure there are no gaps between images. Emboss if desired.

2. Cut close to the outside edge of your repeated images with straight-edge scissors to create a patterned decorative edge.

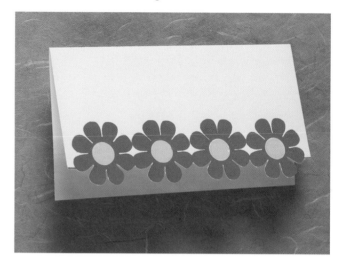

CUT-EDGE LAYERS

1. Cut along all four edges on a piece of card stock. Stamp and decorate as desired.

2. Layer this piece over a slightly larger piece of card stock in a contrasting color and glue in place. Repeat these steps to create as many cut-edge layers as desired.

BORDERS AND FRAMES

Like the various cut edges, borders also enhance a main subject or scene and give your project a finished look. The following are just some of the ways to create borders or frames, using several different methods and materials.

● One of the simplest ways of decorating an edge is to simply draw a straight, thick or thin, line across the edge with a ruler and a marker. This line can be plain or embossed, using an embossing marker. If your line is thick enough, you can also cut along the colored edge with decorative scissors.

● Instead of using a ruler, draw the line freehand for a looser, more whimsical look. You can even draw lines to create borders containing scallops, curlicues, or squiggles! Draw triangles in the corners and fill them in to create faux photo corners.

● Stamp a specially-designed frame, or a combination of corner and border stamps, for quick results. The size of the frame will be more limited, however, with this technique.

HAPPY BIRTHDAY

● Glue a strip of ribbon, decorative trim, or lace to the edge(s) to give a soft, elegant look to your project!

● Masking a border is a simple, yet effective, technique. Choose any stamp with a recognizable image, such as a flower. By stamping only a portion of this image, like the outer petals in this example, the imprint will be unrecognizable and abstract—perfect for repeating along an edge to create a border. The results can be quite surprising and positively striking!

1. Cut a mask in a size much smaller than the outer dimensions of your card. Position and secure the mask in the center of the card.

2. Stamp repeatedly, using an individual image or a combination of images around the exposed area. Stamp off the edges and onto the mask where necessary.

● Sponging color(s) (see page 41) around a mask can create a colorful frame. The sponged color can also be added to a frame already stamped with images.

● Repeat a single image across one or more edges to create an eye-catching border. Try to keep your spacing even. Stamping off the edge can help maintain a balance of images.

● Use a roller stamp to stamp quick borders or a single edge. The long edge of a stamp positioner or a ruler are great guides to use in maintaining a straight line. (see Positioning, page 32).

● Stencil a border using the sponging techniques outlined in Chapter 4 (page 43).

● Try the more elegant look of a hand-torn edge. Hand-tear an edge (or edges) using the methods described on pages 58 and 101, or slowly tear the paper against a metal-edge ruler. Deckle-edge decorative scissors also mimic the look of a hand-torn edge.

● Stamp, or glue cut-out stamped images, in each of the project's four corners. Draw a line, either freehand or with a ruler, connecting the four images into a frame.

● Punch out an edge with a decorative punch. Cut colorful paper strips and use a decorative punch to punch out shapes down the center of the strips. Glue the strips over a contrasting color to create an interesting border. Or, you can punch out shapes and glue the shapes around the edges of a project.

● Hold a piece of card stock at a right angle and run the edges along a pad of embossing ink. (You can also draw an edge freehand using a clear embossing marker.) Dip the wet edges into opaque embossing powder, tap off the excess, and heat.

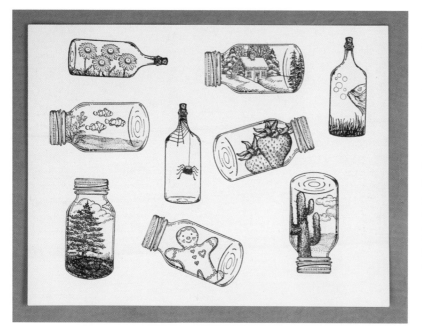

(For more techniques for borders and frames, see pages 67 and 68.)

MORTISE MASKING

Mortise, or reverse, masking is a technique that is used to give the illusion of objects or parts of objects appearing inside other "container" images, such as balloons, jars, or window openings. Stamps that have large enough black centers to fit another image into are suitable for this technique.

28

Although it serves a different purpose, mortise masking works the same as the basic masking technique outlined in Chapter 2. The main difference is that the entire area *outside* of the container image will need to be masked, instead of covering up the actual image you have stamped. A large sheet of scrap paper, therefore, needs to be used to create the mortise mask.

This technique is helpful when placing phrases inside of open images such as banners or phrase balloons. Mortise masking can make precision sponging inside a large open image possible (see page 43).

To create a mortise mask, you'll need:
    Container or jar image rubber stamp
    Rubber stamps with a definite outlined stamp
       image slightly larger than the container image
    Dye ink pad
    Paper or card stock
    Large sheet of scrap paper

1. Stamp a container image onto your scrap paper. Cut the image areas out along the outside of the outline with either an X-acto knife or scissors. Make sure to cut this mortise mask slightly larger than the image.

TIP: MOST CONTAINER IMAGES USED FOR MORTISE MASKING HAVE LARGE BLANK CENTERS, WHICH COMMONLY PRODUCE BACK-PRINTS. IT IS ADVISABLE TO CAREFULLY TRIM THE INSIDE SECTIONS OF YOUR RUBBER TO PREVENT THIS FROM HAPPENING.

2. Stamp the container image onto your project. Let the ink dry. Cover the area outside of this stamped image with your mortise mask.

3. Position your second image and stamp it inside of the cut-out portion of the mortise mask. Stamp a portion of the image onto the mask if necessary.

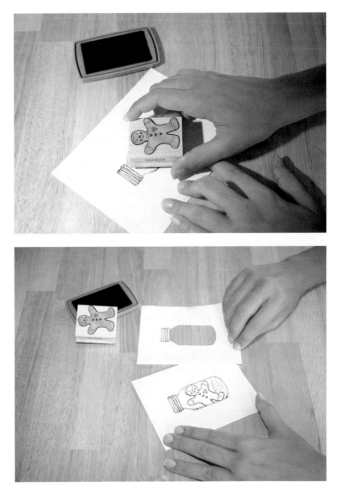

SHADOWING AND MOVEMENT

This technique creates a "fade out" image which suggests movement.

1. Heavily ink your stamp. Stamp the image once onto paper.

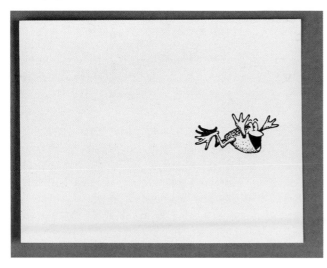

2. Without re-inking the stamp, slightly overlap the back portion of the image and stamp the image again.

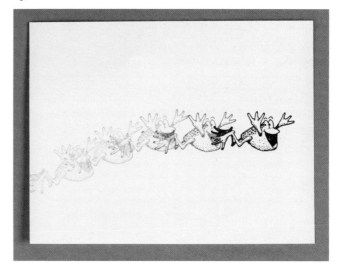

3. Repeat Step 2, positioning the stamp further back each time, until there is no more ink left on the stamp.

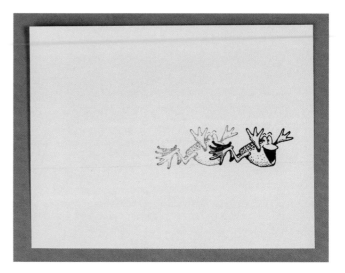

You can mask a main portion of a stamp so that only one part, such as a paw or tail, will show the suggestion of movement.

This interesting shadow effect can be achieved by stamping an image in one color and then over-stamping it in a second color. The second image should be slightly "off" of the first image. Try this double-image shadow technique using blue and red inks. When viewed with 3-D glasses, the image will appear to pop out!

30

MIRROR IMAGING

This technique allows you to imprint a reverse image of your original stamp image. It can be used in creating scenes or when you want identical images to face each other. Mirror imaging can also be when the image appearing on the stamp has been drawn facing the wrong direction for your particular need. A special large, flat rubber stamp that contains no image is used for this technique. If you prefer, try using a large eraser, children's play putty, or even a brayer rolled over the top of an inked stamp.

1. Press a well-inked stamp image onto the rubber side of the mirror-image stamp.

2. Quickly press the inked image onto a piece of paper.

TIP: WHEN USING A STAMP POSITIONER, MAKE SURE THE IMAGES ALREADY STAMPED ON YOUR PROJECT ARE COMPLETELY DRY (OR COOLED DOWN FROM EMBOSSING). OTHERWISE, THE TISSUE OR ACETATE USED FOR POSITIONING YOUR NEXT IMAGE WILL SMEAR THE INK OR MELTED EMBOSSING POWDER WHEN PLACED OVER THE PROJECT.

POSITIONING IMAGES

The most accurate way of aligning images involves a method using tracing paper (a heavy grade works best) and a special L- or T-shaped tool called a stamp positioner. There are several versions of this tool on the market, but you can make your own version by nailing or screwing two 6" or longer pieces of wood together in an "L" or "T" shape. If you choose to make your own tool, however, be sure it is at least 1/2" thick and forms a perfect 90° angle.

Individual pieces of tracing paper cut into squares or rectangles (with 90° angles) are used for each separate stamp image. When the project is completed, the used tracing paper pieces can be filed and used for another project that incorporates the same images. Although the stamped image will dry slower on sheets of Mylar or acetate, they also work as well as tracing paper and have the advantage of being easily cleaned off and reused, so one sheet can be used for many images.

This technique is helpful when restamping over an image that did not stamp well or for maintaining a straight line of images in a border.

These frames were created by stamping four identical corner stamp images. The image on the left appears to be a single, perfectly-aligned frame, thanks to help from a stamp positioner. The images on the right, however, were all carefully stamped by eye. Note the slight misalignment and gaps in between images.

To position a stamp, you'll need:
- Wood-mounted rubber stamp
- Dye ink pad
- Paper or card stock
- Stamp positioner
- Tracing paper (or sheet of Mylar)

1. Stamp an image on your project and set aside. Line up a corner of the tracing paper to fit exactly into the positioner's right angle. (Note: Write the word "Top" on the tracing paper before you begin. This will prevent placing the paper upside-down and lining it up against the wrong corner in Step 2.)

2. Ink your stamp. Bring the wood mount into the right angle, flush against the positioner. Press and stamp the image onto the tracing paper. Let dry.

3. Place the stamped tracing paper on top of the project exactly where you want the finished image to be.

4. Line up the positioner against the same corner of the tracing paper as in Step 1. Leaving the positioner in place, remove the tracing paper. Line up your inked stamp against the positioner, as in Step 2, and press it onto your project.

Chapter 4

Let There Be Color

Color is phenomenal! Reflecting our personalities and our moods, color affects how we interpret everything we see—it breathes life into a world that is drawn in shades of gray. When the sky is baby blue and the leaves are a soft shade of green, it must be spring! But, if the sky is steel blue and the leaves are brown, red, orange, and yellow, the chill of autumn is in the air!

Color adds a whole new dimension to a stamped outline image. Depending on which color techniques or materials you choose, you can transform even an ordinary birthday card into a work of art! From the broad, flat colors of contemporary design to the subtle look of watercolor, color can definitely make an impact on your stamped projects.

There is no one right coloring technique to choose above the others except in matching the appropriate materials to the correct coloring techniques. Use of the different coloring techniques outlined below is a matter of personal preference, skill, ability, and, most of all, confidence. As you explore the world of color, keep in mind that color is a form of expression applicable to all ages and personalities.

COLOR INK PADS

One of the quickest ways of adding color to a stamped piece is by stamping the images in different colored inks. This technique is best used with solid images or simple outlines and greetings. Just remember to clean the stamp each time you change ink colors!

Although ink pads offer a wide spectrum of color, most of their effects are limited to use on solid images. No matter how colorful the ink is used to stamp them, outline images remain just that—outlines. However, something positively magical happens when color is added to these stamped images!

Colored inks add visual excitement to this simple, but expressive, birthday card.

NOTE: THERE ARE MANY FINE ART AND DESIGN BOOKS AVAILABLE IN BOOK, ART SUPPLY STORES AND LIBRARIES TO HELP YOU UNDERSTAND THE PRINCIPLES OF COLOR THEORY. THESE CAN TAKE MUCH OF THE MYSTERY OUT OF THE USE OF COLOR FOR THE NOVICE, AS WELL AS REFRESH THE MORE EXPERIENCED ARTIST.

MARKERS

These are staples in coloring tools for rubber stamp artists. Markers come in different inks, widths, and tips to cover a variety of different applications. As is the case with many supplies mentioned throughout this book, superior results are made possible by superior materials. This is 100 percent true when choosing which markers to use.

With children's stamping projects, safety and practicality are of utmost importance. Washable, nontoxic markers are the most suitable for children. However, for the more sophisticated rubber stamp artist, a better-, or even professional-, quality water-based, non-solvent marker is essential.

Water-soluble, dye-based markers are the most popular markers used to color in stamped images, because they are easy to use for coloring in small areas, blending, and shading and they come in a complete array of colors. Although these markers offer superb results on white and light-colored papers, they usually do not show up on darker surfaces. And, because they are dye-based, the colors will tend to fade over time when exposed to light. Pigment markers are the best choice for black and other hard-to-color papers. They come in a full range of colors, including many dazzling metallics. Some of these permanent markers, however, might be solvent-based and should be used with proper ventilation.

TIP: PERMANENT MARKERS SHOULD NEVER BE USED TO COLOR DIRECTLY ONTO YOUR STAMPS!

WARNING: READ LABELS AND USE CAUTION WHEN SOLVENT-BASED ART TOOLS ARE USED BY CHILDREN OR CHEMICALLY-SENSITIVE INDIVIDUALS!

Additional marker applications include:
● Embossed image outlines make marker coloring a breeze. Because the image is raised, it forms a resist. This makes it very easy to color within the lines, thus speeding up the coloring process.
● Use markers to touch up solid areas that did not imprint well due to improper inking of the stamp, pressure, or paper texture.
● When markers begin to dry up, they can be used for a dry brush technique or as a blending tool.

Coloring Directly on a Stamp

1. Color directly on a rubber stamp with water-based brush markers.

2. Breathe heavily onto the rubber and quickly press the stamp onto a piece of paper or card stock.

NOTE: Breathing onto the rubber remoistens the marker ink, which may begin to partially dry before you finish coloring the entire image.

This technique allows you to color different portions of a stamp with the colors of your choice. This is especially useful if you want to isolate a specific part of a stamp to imprint in a different color or when creating your own rainbow combinations. You can also use this technique when you want to stamp using just a portion of your rubber stamp image. This technique can be especially dynamic when using solid image stamps on glossy, coated white card stock.

Water-based Brush Markers

The style of marker you choose will depend on what they will be used for. The wide, flat brush markers, with their vibrant colors and stiff applicator tips, are the perfect choice for coloring directly on stamps, especially large, solid ones. These large markers offer control while also providing the ability to color large areas quickly. The vibrancy of these markers is most apparent when stamped on glossy stock.

In addition to isolating image areas on a stamp and coloring different portions of a stamp with specific colors, you can also blend colors directly on the stamps for extra pizzazz.

From top to bottom: permanent markers, embossing marker, brush marker, kid's marker, and dual-tip markers.

FRUITY NOTE CARD

MATERIALS

Grapes and cherry image rubber stamps*
Fuschia, ultramarine, hunter green, red, and deep pink dye-
    based brush markers
Glossy note card

Used in this project: *#FT-43 Cherry and #1210 Grapes (Marks of Distinction)

1. Color the rubber image portion of the grape stamp using
the brush markers. Use the lighter color (fuschia) first.
Quickly color the darker shade (ultramarine) in a few spots
for shading and blend the colors together with the lighter
marker.

2. Breathe heavily onto the colored rubber, as described on page 35.

3. Immediately stamp the image onto the note card.

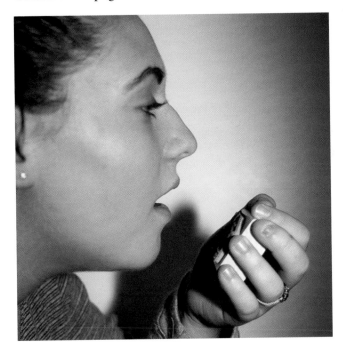

4. Continue stamping both of the images, blending and shading colors where desired and isolating areas of color where needed.

Double-Tipped Watercolor Brush Markers

Narrow, double-tipped watercolor brush markers allow the stamp artist to color in small areas easily and blend colors in larger areas of a stamped image. Marker blending is achieved by applying two or more colors from a similar palette or color group (i.e., yellow, yellow-orange, and orange) side-by-side or in layers on the stamped image. The marker tip is in a shape similar to a watercolor brush. Colors are blended together by working one color gently into the other, using the marker tip as you would a brush.

Always begin with the lighter color(s), gradually blending the darker color(s) into it. Avoid "scrubbing" the paper or the surface will begin to fray. More dramatic color effects over larger areas can be accomplished using a special blending marker. This marker is colorless and is used only for blending. As you become more familiar with marker blending, try your hand at shading using complementary colors, a wider palette of color combinations, or grays.

TWO-STEP BLENDING OF SIMPLE COLORS (LILY CARD)

MATERIALS

Large outline flower image rubber stamp*
Black permanent dye ink pad**
Double-tipped watercolor brush markers in several shades of green, pink, coral, and red***
White matte note card
Optional: colorless blending marker

Used in this project: *#A1660G Lily (Rubber Stampede) **#58 Jet Black Impress Raised Dye Inkpad (Tsukineko) ***Dual Brush-Pen markers (Tombow) in the following colors: #138, #158, #171, #173, #800, #823, and #837

1. Stamp the flower image in black. Let the ink dry completely.

2. Beginning with the lightest shades, color in the areas of the flower and leaves as shown.

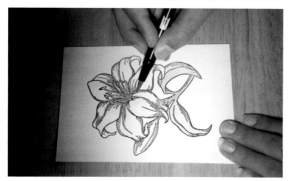

3. Gradually add touches of darker tones and blend these into the lighter areas with the lighter color marker or a colorless blending marker.

TIP: IF THE BRUSH TIP OF YOUR MARKER BECOMES STAINED WHEN BLENDING COLORS, REMOVE THE EXCESS COLOR BY SIMPLY "DRAWING" IT OFF ON SCRAP PAPER!

WATERCOLOR BLENDING (CHAMELEON CARD)

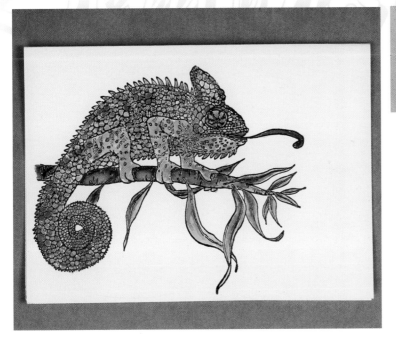

WATERCOLOR BLENDING TECHNIQUE

This is an interesting watercolor effect that can be achieved with a technique that involves using marker pigment as you would watercolor.

MATERIALS

Large lizard outline rubber stamp*
Permanent black dye ink pad, preferably one made especially for watercolor
Assorted water-based markers
White note card or watercolor paper cut to the correct size and scored to create a fold
Plastic palette or foam tray, small paintbrush, water containers

Used in this project: *#K958 Lizard on a Limb (Red Hot Rubber!, Inc.)

1. Stamp the lizard on the note card or paper. Let dry completely.

2. Scribble markers onto a plastic palette or foam tray.

3. Touch the marker scribble with a small, damp paintbrush to pick up some of the pigment. (The wetter the brush, the more diluted or lighter the color will be.)

4. Apply the color to the stamped image, blending the colors as shown to create a watercolor look, or wet the surface you will be coloring first to create a more subtle washed look.

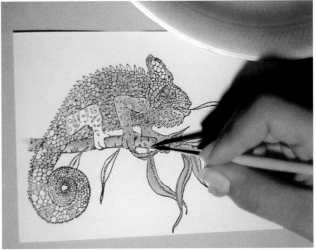

TIP: KEEP TWO SMALL CONTAINERS OF CLEAN WATER HANDY, ONE FOR "PAINTING" THE COLORS, AND THE OTHER FOR CLEANING THE PAINTBRUSH BETWEEN COLOR CHANGES.

WATERCOLOR AND WATER-COLOR PENCILS

Watercolors take some time to master, but the results will be well worth the effort. Practice on scrap paper until you feel comfortable with the medium. And, as with other techniques in this book, the correct combination of materials, supplies, and techniques are essential.

When using watercolor or watercolor pencils, make sure you stamp your design on watercolor paper. Most other papers commonly used for stamping will warp when they get wet. Watercolor paper comes in pads or sheets of cold or hot pressed paper. Hot pressed is the smoother of the two and is a better surface for stamping on. Watercolor paper contains sizing to prevent the fibers from absorbing too much water. This distinctive quality helps keep the intensity of color on the surface of the paper. Choose a light- to medium-weight paper for most rubber-stamped projects.

You will need to use permanent ink for stamping images that will be watercolored. Some ink pads state that they are suitable for watercolor, but because most dye ink tends to bleed when moistened, you will need to test its degree of permanence on scrap paper. Let the ink dry at least 1 hour before coloring the image in. Fabric and pigment inks are more permanent and water resistant, but they dry very slowly. Embossing over these two inks will eliminate the problem with bleeding and dry these inks quickly. Test the paper first, however, to make sure it will withstand the heat without warping.

NOTE: WATERCOLOR IS NOT APPLICABLE FOR FABRIC PROJECTS THAT WILL BE WASHED.

Watercolors come in tubes, bottles of dyes, or in solid cakes. Choosing between them is a matter of preference, degree of quality desired, and expense. It is important to use a watercolor brush with these paints. These brushes are specially shaped to hold the aqueous paint and give greater control when painting.

Watercolor paint can be applied directly to dry paper with the full intensity of color or added to moistened paper to create a wash (diluted pigment). This medium needs a quick hand! One key to successful watercolor painting is to work rapidly and not allow your paper surface to dry until you are finished applying and blending colors. Unlike acrylics or oils, which require a more controlled application, watercolor is a looser medium to work in.

Watercolor pencils release color when water is applied to them, making them relatively easy to use. While the results will resemble watercolor when moistened, the pencils still retain their linear quality when used as a colored pencil. The more layers of pigment you lay down, the more intense the released colors will be when moistened.

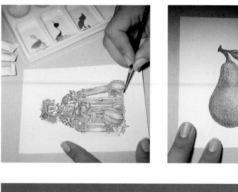

The scarecrow on the left is an example of how watercolor can change a stamped image. Although you can still see subtle pencil strokes, the watercolor pencil used on the pear image also creates a similar realistic look.

40

COLORED PENCILS

Colored pencils have a softer look than markers, and because they rely on the layering of colors to achieve the end result, colored pencils can be a very forgiving medium to use. Colored pencils obtain their distinctive appearance by applying layer upon layer of pigment onto paper. You can find colored pencils in a range of quality and price, from the inexpensive school grade to the highest professional quality. While glossy stock is unsuitable for colored pencils, they can be used effectively on most other papers. Different paper textures, however, will affect how the colored pencil actually is laid down on the paper, resulting in correspondingly different looks. Rougher textured paper will result in a "toothier" pencil stroke, while on smoother papers, colored pencil can achieve a more "painterly" quality.

This repeat pattern was stamped on white cardstock to keep the colors true when the images were colored in. The bright background was sponged in, using dye ink pads and stamping sponges.

SPONGING

A very simple technique that is easily mastered, sponging involves applying ink from an ink pad or marker onto a surface using a dabbing motion and a small sponge. This stamping favorite can help create very interesting effects, especially for backgrounds. Brush markers tend to show lines or streaks when coloring in large areas, whereas sponging color onto a background or around stamped images offers a streak-free way of adding color and can help add drama to many projects. When used as an accent around multiple images in a busy pattern, a single sponged color can help reduce the feeling of chaos and add cohesiveness to the design. The alternate ways to achieve a more even effect is to either mask over the stamped images and sponge color onto the entire background area, or to stroke marker onto a sponge and lightly blend some of the streaks away.

Stamping sponges come in a variety of shapes, including triangular wedges, round, and a small bullet shape with an attached handle. Because triangular cosmetic sponges can leave a distinct edge mark, it is preferable to use a smooth-textured round sponge or stenciling tool when trying this technique, but you can try squeezing and holding up the edges of the triangular sponge so that the sponging surface is more rounded. Make sure to use a different sponge for each color ink you use.

SPONGING AND MASKING

You can create a starburst, streaked background or border with sponging and masking.

To do this, you'll need:
Dye ink pads in three or more
   solid colors
Stamping sponges (one sponge
   for each color ink)
White note card with an image
   already stamped in the
   center
Scrap paper or Post-it note

1. Mask the center of a stamped note card with a small rectangular mask.

2. Dab one of the sponges several times on one of the ink pads.

3. Beginning in the center of the mask, sponge this color onto the remaining exposed portion of the note card by pulling the colored sponge toward the outer edges of the card. Repeat all around the card, applying color from the center out, leaving enough white space for the additional two colors.

4. Repeat Steps 2 and 3 for each of the remaining ink pad colors, using a clean sponge for each color.

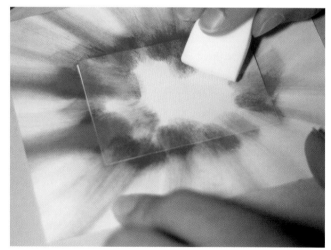

42

Various projects and the stencils used to create them.

SPONGING AND STENCILING

Using stencils as "masks," sponging and stenciling can create the illusion of waves, clouds, mountains, and sandy beaches! This technique simply involves sponging ink along the edge of a patterned stencil. You can use a single color or blended combinations for the entire background or you can create wild rainbow looks by changing colors each time you move the stencil. Stenciling is actually a form of masking (and vice versa). You can create a stencil, use a ready-made stencil, or use items such as lace to create interesting patterns. Commercially-made Mylar stencils clean up very easily and come in a variety of pre-cut edges and shapes. If you are artistic, you can, of course, cut your own stencils from card stock or sheets of acetate. Cut shapes such as rectangles, hearts, and ovals to use as border templates, or create edging such as waves or clouds. As with cutting masks, make sure to cut several stencils at a time. These multiples will come in handy so that you can use a different stencil sheet for each different color. This way, the ink color already on the stencil won't transfer onto the sponge or project.

WINTER SCENE DOOR HANGER

MATERIALS

Small snowflake and winter
   silhouette image rubber stamps*
Teal, black, emerald green, light blue,
   and purple dye ink pads**
Glossy white door hanger or glossy
   white paper cut to shape
Pre-made Mylar or hand-cut card
   stock stencils in the shape of
   trees and clouds***
Stamping sponges

Used in this project: *#A212 Solitary Snowflake (Hero
Arts) and #H-1275 Sleigh Ride Silhouette (Maine
Street Stamps) **#58 Jet Black, #11 Emerald, #75
Sky Mist, #07 Pansy, and #10 Teal Impress Raised
Dye Inkpads (Tsukineko) ***#92 MTN Mountain
View Stamp Art Template (All Night Media, Inc.)
and a hand-cut cloud stencil

1. Position the cloud template about 1/2" below the top edge of the door hanger. Gently sponge light blue ink against the template edge. Sponge over the same area with purple ink.

2. Moving the template down and over, reposition the clouds. Repeat sponging the blue and purple inks. Continue sponging clouds until half of the project is covered.

3. Switch templates to sponge trees. Sponge alternating teal blue and green rows of trees until you reach 1" above the bottom edge.

4. Sponge snowbanks by sponging light blue ink against the cloud template. Let the ink dry completely.

5. Overprint the silhouette stamp image in black. Randomly stamp snowflakes in teal.

BRAYERING COLOR

A brayer is a tool made to cover wide areas with color. Resembling a paint roller, this tool can be made of rubber, hard foam, or a soft sponge-like material. A brayer can be used to apply different background patterns by applying ink to the roller and then rolling the brayer across the stamping surface. The different effects achieved by using a brayer are a direct result of the different methods of applying color to the brayer.

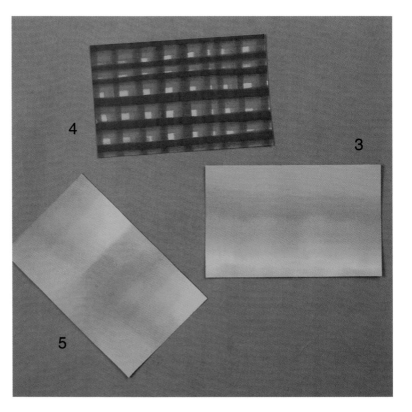

• (1) Rolling a brayer over an ink pad is the quickest way to apply one color to a background. Roll the brayer over the pad several times until it is completely inked. (2) Then roll the inked brayer across paper or another stamping surface. Continue rolling until all of the ink has been transferred from the roller to the stamping surface.

• Remove any streaks by repeatedly rolling, overlapping your strokes until you get the desired color intensity and shade.

• (3) Roll a small brayer over a rainbow ink pad several times, completely coating the roller. Roll the color onto your surface in one direction. Repeat until all of the ink is off the brayer.

• (4 and 5) Try rolling the brayer in two different directions with a rainbow-inked brayer to create a rainbow plaid.

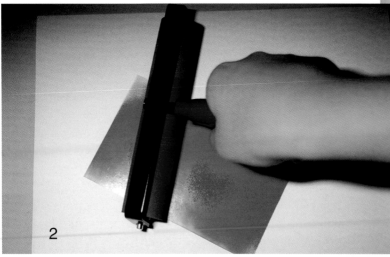

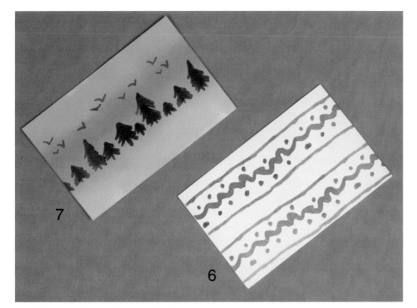

● (6) Another option is to draw patterns on the brayer with any type of marker. By changing the direction you apply the marker color onto your surface, you can create color background patterns such as plaids and rainbow confetti.

● (7) You can also draw simple silhouette shapes onto the roller, such as trees or birds, and roll out a scene!

● (8) Stamp an image using clear embossing ink on white paper and emboss in white or clear. Watch your images appear when you brayer color over them!

● (9) Brayer an interesting background. Stamp and emboss solid stamp images onto the background when it is dry, using opaque pigment ink, or embossing ink and embossing powder.

● (10) Brayer patterns or rainbow colors inside a mortise-masked image. Make sure your mask protects the entire project.

● (11) Create plaids and rainbow patterns by rolling a rainbow-inked brayer directly onto solid image stamps. Stamp immediately onto glossy paper.

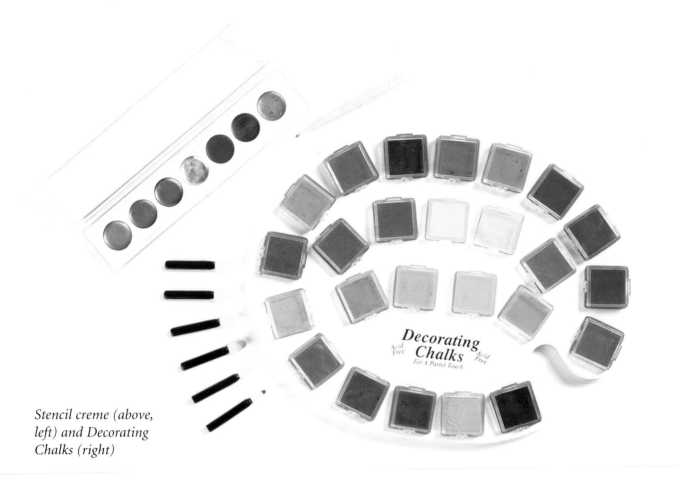

Stencil creme (above, left) and Decorating Chalks (right)

ADDITIONAL COLORING MATERIALS

In addition to the materials above, there are several other ways of adding color to a stamped image or project, including chalks, stencil creme, textile markers, metallic pens, and fabric paints, among others.

Chalk or pastels, dabbed onto your project with a cotton swab, make delicate coloring tools for non-fabric surfaces. Use a fixative to keep the chalks or pastels from smearing or rubbing onto other surfaces. Check fixative labels for correct use and warnings!

The texture of stencil creme is similar to that of lipstick. These creme colors dry slowly, blend easily, and can be applied to a stamped image with their special sponge applicators and then sealed by embossing with clear embossing powder.

Vibrantly-colored textile markers are specially formulated to work on fabric. These markers are generally permanent and can be used on a variety of other surfaces, including leather, wood, and paper.

Although some of these markers need to be heat-set (see page 103), they are ideal for use when a greater degree of permanence is required. Make sure to follow manufacturers' directions and seal properly on leather, as advised (see page 113).

Silver and gold metallic pens can be used to create elegant gold- or silver-finished touches. White correction pens add white highlights quickly and easily to colored or dark surfaces. And don't forget that you can add color to embossed images with embossing markers and emboss with clear or pearl powders.

Some of the paints and markers used with fabric stamping can also be used on other surfaces. Mix fabric paints or acrylics with their appropriate mediums to offer boldness and permanence to other surfaces, such as wood. Fabric paints may remain tacky, however, if applied in high humidity.

What a brilliant statement this simple floral basket note card (top right) makes with the added sparkle of glitter glue! The delicate softness of the decorative chalks used on the morning glories note card (bottom right) contrasts against the vibrancy of the textile markers used to create the lily doily (left). Projects on the right designed by Deb Parks.

EMBELLISHMENTS

Try adding color with embellishments. Dimensional paints, puffy paint, glitter, or glitter glue will add spots of color that can jazz up many projects. For extra richness and depth, apply glitter glue over stamped images that have already been colored in with markers.

PUTTING IT ALL TOGETHER: COMBINING MULTIPLE STAMP IMAGES WITH MULTIPLE TECHNIQUES

The same rules for design and composition used in traditional art forms apply when choosing multiple images for a project. For example, when creating a simple card, begin with the one stamp that is to be the focal point of the design. Add other stamp images, such as background textures, phrases, or small images that repeat well, or try choosing image combinations around a theme. Varying the sizes of the images you use will help maintain balance in your composition.

Experiment with image combinations to discover which images work best together. Different combinations—and colors—create different moods or statements. Sometimes the most unlikely combinations can also be the most striking!

At some point, you will want to begin combining both multiple images and multiple techniques. That is how scenes are created. The realistic effects in the project demonstration that follows are a result of combining stamp images, masking, repeat design, sponging and color techniques, and shadow and movement. The more confident you become with your skills, the more techniques you will utilize with each successive project.

PROJECT DEMONSTRATION:
A REALISTIC SCENE

MATERIALS

Horses, trees, grass, hills, and clouds rubber stamps*
Black dye ink pad
Assorted colors of double-tipped watercolor brush markers
8-1/2 x 11 sheet of white paper
Scrap paper
Straight-edge scissors

*Used in this project: #C457 Beach Grass, #LL263 Gifts of Nature Horse Set (Hero Arts Rubber
Stamps, Inc.); #452E Clouds, #451H Oak Tree, #453H Pine Forest, #186H Running Horses,
#465G Fir Tree, #181E Galloping Horse (All Night Media, Inc.); #C1308 Fir (Maine Street
Stamps); #G018 Sand/Snow (Stampendous, Inc.)

1. Practice stamping each image separately and in combinations on a piece of scrap paper. Stamp and cut out masks for the images that will appear in front of others.

2. Begin with the front or the portion of the scene that is the closest to the viewer. Using only the top portion of the tree stamp, create "bushes" in the lower right-hand corner, by stamping off the edges of the paper. Create and place a mask over one of the bushes as shown and stamp a horse pair behind it. Begin adding more trees and scenery.

3. Continue adding layers to your scene, masking the horse to add a repeat design row of grass. Stamp a single running horse as shown, using the shadowing and movement technique. Continue masking and repeating images, stamping off the edges where necessary.

4. Complete your scene by adding horses behind the trees. Adding details such as clouds and hills will help define a horizon and a sky.

5. Add the final touches to your scene by coloring it in with markers, colored pencil, or any of the other methods described in this chapter.

Chapter 5
Paper Crafts

Above: The wide range of paper products available for stamp art projects continues to grow each year. Right: Elaborate paper layers with decorative edges. Project designed by Barbara Barnes for All Night Media.

Left: Black triangles were cut out and glued on to create the illusion of photo corners on this simple card.

The majority of rubber stamping is performed on paper of one sort or another. This is the first surface most people begin with when they try their hand at artistic rubber stamping. It is important, therefore, to spend some time getting familiar with some of the many types of paper available.

Paper is available in a variety of colors, styles, and textures—from exotic, roughly-textured handmade paper to smooth, finely-milled types. The finish can be coarse or smooth, glossy or matte. Paper texture can affect the way an image will stamp. The smoother the surface, the sharper the image.

Paper can be either coated or non-coated. Coated papers (including glossy Kromekote and many matte note card stocks) are less absorbent than non-coated (like handmade, rice, and various stationary papers). Ink stays on the surface of coated paper because the coating prevents it from penetrating into the paper's fibers. This feature can dramatically increase the image's clarity and its color's vibrancy, but it also increases the drying time of any image stamped on coated stock. Images stamped with pigment ink should always be embossed when using glossy-coated stock or they will take forever (literally) to dry! Embossing on glossy-coated paper dries and seals the pigment ink, but the intense heat from the embossing tool also tends to warp and scorch it. Make sure your heat source is a little further away when embossing on this type of paper.

Non-coated papers are, conversely, more absorbent than the coated varieties. Images stamped on this type of paper dry more rapidly. But, if the paper is too absorbent, the stamped images might lose some of their sharpness, because the ink might bleed too easily into the fibers; this is especially true with paper that contains cotton fibers.

The best way to choose paper to stamp on is to experiment. Individual images will stamp differently on different papers, just as the different inks will perform differently from one paper type to another. Test your ink and markers on a scrap of paper first to determine which supplies (and images) work the best on individual paper stocks. Neutral- or light-colored papers are the easiest to work with because most colored inks and coloring tools will show up well on them. Darker or brightly-colored papers, however, provide a rich contrast for metallic, opaque, white, or neon embossing powders.

Much of the complexity in this elegant card is a result of multiple layers of different-colored and -shaped paper.

Most retail stores or mail-order companies selling rubber stamp supplies carry an assortment of quality stamping and decorative papers. Acid- and lignan-free archival-quality papers can be purchased for projects that include photographs (see page 66). Although some papers might prove unsuitable for stamping, they might be perfect for layering or collage effects. Much of the pleasure derived from rubber stamping is from the surprise discoveries made through the creative exploration of materials, supplies, and techniques!

These two cards above demonstrate how the same images can seem so different when layered using varying methods. The dancing couple on the left is attached to a black square slightly larger than the top layer. Four small black triangles have been cut out and glued on top, to simulate a framed photo. Punched-out star confetti echo the stars in the layered background print. The card on the right incorporates layering the main stamped image over two angled rectangles and a simple background repeat. The corrugated paper adds textural interest.

The card at left illustrates randomly hand-torn colored paper layers, whereas the bookmark at right incorporates layers that were cut more precisely on a paper cutter.

LAYERING WITH PAPER

Layering papers with contrasting colors and textures is an easy, yet dramatic, way of adding interest to even the simplest paper projects. Different paper layers can form a frame around a single stamped image or masked scene, drawing attention to it and act as a tool to help transform a plain project into a more dynamic one.

Layering can include papers that have each been stamped with different images. Crimped paper, torn tissue, lace doilies, or paper cut with decorative-edge scissors are all examples of some unusual textures used for layering.

PROJECT DEMONSTRATION:
LAYERED PEACOCK NOTE CARD

MATERIALS

Peacock feather rubber stamp*
Marble-textured three-sided stamp or other
    background texture image
Green and black dye ink pads**
Clear embossing ink pad
Black pigment ink pad
Clear sparkle and gold embossing powders
Watercolor brush markers***
White, black, and green card stock
Tan note card
Heat tool, scissors, glue or adhesive

Used in this project: *#TC01 Marble Texture Cube (Stampendous, Inc.)
and #J902 Peacock Feather (Red Hot Rubber!, Inc.) **#58 Jet Black and
#11 Emerald Impress Raised Dye Inkpads (Tsukineko) ***Dual Brush-
Pen Markers (Tombow) in the following colors: #195, #452, and #991

1. Stamp the marble texture (or other background
texture image) onto the tan note card using green
dye ink. Repeat the texture background over the
entire card. Over-stamp the entire background with
black dye ink, using a different image side of the
cube.

2. Stamp a peacock feather onto the black card
stock using clear embossing ink. Emboss with gold
embossing powder. Cut a 3-1/4" x 4-1/4" rectangle
around the image. Cut a 3-1/2" x 4-1/2" rectangle
from the green card stock.

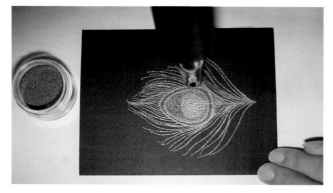

3. Stamp a feather image onto the white card stock,
using black pigment ink, and emboss with clear
sparkle powder. Cut out the eye of the feather and
color it in with markers as shown.

4. Glue the cut-out eye onto the black card, over
the image already stamped on it. Center and attach
the black and green cards in layers onto the marble-
stamped card using glue or adhesive.

LAIR-ED TIGER PICTURE

MATERIALS

Large tiger, paw print, and tiger print background rubber stamps*
Black dye ink pad
Watercolor brush markers**
Clear embossing ink pad
Opaque black or brown embossing powder
5" x 5-1/4" white glossy card stock
8-1/2" x 11" sheet of black mat board or
   card stock
7-3/8" x 8" piece of light tan card stock or
   paper
7-3/4" x 8-1/2" piece of medium tan card
   stock or paper
8-1/2" square piece of dark tan card stock
   or paper
Heat tool, scissors, glue and double-stick
   tape or pressure-sensitive adhesive***,
   pencil, stamping sponge
Optional: X-acto knife, metal ruler

Used in this project: *#A8555E Tiger Print (Rubber Stampede), #221C
Cat's Paw (All Night Media, Inc.), #K954 Jungle Cat (Red Hot Rubber!,
Inc.) **Dual-Brush Pen Markers (Tombow) in the following colors:
#N77, #N89, #025, #055, #076, #098, #126, #133, #158, #796, #823, #912,
#933, and #947 ***PeelnStick Press On Adhesive (Therm O Web)

NOTE: BOTH THE BLACK PAPER STOCK AND
THE EMBOSSING POWDER CAN VARY IN COLOR,
DEPENDING ON YOUR SOURCE. YOU MIGHT
WANT TO EXPERIMENT WITH OTHER POSSIBILI-
TIES, SUCH AS A DARK-COLORED PIGMENT INK
PAD AND CLEAR POWDER. ANOTHER OPTION IS
TO USE ONE OF THE DARKER, MORE UNUSUAL
EMBOSSING POWDER COLORS OR MIXTURES.
FOR MORE INFORMATION ON EMBOSSING VARI-
ATIONS, SEE CHAPTER 7.

1. Using the black dye ink, stamp the tiger in the
center of the glossy white card stock. Allow the ink
to dry thoroughly.

2. Stamp the tiger print background repeatedly
onto the dark tan card stock, using black dye ink. Let
dry. Gently hand-tear an edge around all four sides,
about 1" in from the edge, pulling toward yourself as
you tear.

3. Cut four 5/8" x 2-1/2" strips from the scraps left
from Step 2. Glue these strips to the corners of the
stamped tiger square, on angles as shown. Trim off
the excess.

4. Using clear embossing ink and opaque black or brown embossing powder, stamp and emboss paw prints on the black mat board or card stock.

5. Lightly sponge black dye ink around the edges of the medium tan card stock or paper. Center and attach to the black embossed board with double-stick tape or pressure-sensitive adhesive. Attach a 7-3/8" x 8" piece of light tan card stock or paper over these layers. Angle the tiger print piece as shown and attach this layer as well, leaving the corners loose. Position and attach the tiger square onto the tiger print piece. Curl the loose edges of the torn paper layer around a pencil.

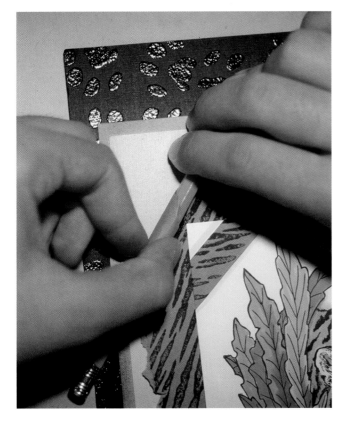

6. Color the tiger image with watercolor brush markers, blending where desired (see page 37). Add trompe l'oeil touches (see page 99) with a light gray marker around the tiger, lower leaves, and along the four tiger print corner strips.

7. Optional easel back: Cut out a strip of mat board that measures 3-1/2" x 11". Measure and lightly score a straight line 2" from one short edge using an X-acto knife against a metal ruler. Do not cut all of the way through the board. Attach the easel back strip to the back of the stamped picture, 1" below the top edge, using a piece of double-stick tape or pressure-sensitive adhesive along the top 2" section of the easel back strip.

Daisy Bonnet Card and Lined and Stamped Envelope

Project designed by Deb Parks

ENVELOPES

A magnificently-stamped card needs an equally impressive envelope to match! Enve-lopes come ready-made in sizes to match most note cards, but you can make your own using special envelope templates. Lined envelopes can be particularly striking, especially when lined in a contrasting stamped paper.

MATERIALS

Daisy border or single image daisy and hat rubber stamps*
Black dye ink pad**
Watercolor brush markers***
4" x 5-1/4" matching note card and envelope
Two sheets (3-1/4" x 4-1/4" and 8-1/2" x 11") of vanilla-colored paper
Scrap of white card stock
Ruler, scissors, glue stick, adhesive foam, clothing steamer or tea kettle

Used in this project: *#2401 Floral Set (All Night Media, Inc.) and #A1603E Garden Hat (Rubber Stampede) **#58 Jet Black Impress Raised Dye Inkpad (Tsukineko) ***Dual Brush-Pen Markers (Tombow) in the following colors: #N15, #061, #133, #195, #533, #970, #990, and #991

1. **Stamp the card:** Stamp vertical rows of daisies on the 3-1/4" x 4-1/4" piece of vanilla-colored paper. Mask and stamp off the edges where necessary. Draw a thin black line around all four edges of the paper. Stamp the hat image on the scrap piece of card stock. Cut the hat out and color as desired with watercolor brush markers. Glue the daisy-stamped paper onto the 4" x 5-1/4" note card with a glue stick. Attach the hat to the center of the daisy-stamped paper with a small piece of adhesive foam.

2. **Create the lining paper for the inside of the envelope:** Gently steam open the envelope pocket with a clothing steamer or tea kettle and let it dry. Using your envelope as a template, trace the outer shape onto a piece of scrap paper. Measure in 3/8" from the edges of the envelope flap and redraw your template edges for the flap portion only (this will allow the glued edge of the envelope flap to remain exposed when the lining is attached to the inside of the envelope). Trace the template outline onto a

piece of vanilla-colored paper to match the note card and cut it out to create a lining paper to stamp on.

3. **Stamp the outside of the envelope:** Lay the envelope face up and open. Stamp the daisy border completely around the edge. Mask as necessary to create a continuous border of flowers. Color with watercolor brush markers as desired.

4. **Stamping the lining paper:** Stamp rows of daisies as before in the lower portion of the lining paper, below the flap section. Stamping off the edge, stamp portions of the daisy image in the flap corners as shown. Stamp a hat in the center of the flap area and color in the images with markers.

5. **Complete the envelope:** Glue the stamped lining paper onto the inside of the envelope with a glue stick. Refold the envelope and reglue the sides of the envelope pocket to close.

Papier Mâché

Stamping on paper does not need to be limited to note cards or bookmarks. Papier mâché boxes, frames, or other flat novelty items make ideal surfaces to stamp on. Just seal the porous surface first with a colorful layer of acrylic paint before stamping.

NOTE: Papier mâché and other paper boxes will "give" as you apply pressure with your stamp. In order to have a rigid, flat surface to stamp against, place a piece of wood, hard plastic, or another smaller hard, flat surface under the box lid or inside of the box when stamping. When stamping the sides of an oval or circular box, use the fingers of your free hand to apply counter pressure inside of the box as you stamp onto the outside curved surface.

PAPIER MÂCHÉ ANGEL BOX

MATERIALS

Small star and outline angel rubber stamps*
White and lavender acrylic paint**
Black pigment ink pad
Clear embossing ink pad
Clear and silver embossing powders
Watercolor brush markers***
Fine-point white correction pen
Oval papier mâché box
Stamping sponges, heat tool

Used in this project: *#A127 Shining Star and #G-126 Guardian Angel (Maine Street Stamps) **#OC156 Medium Lavender Aleene's Premium-Coat Acrylic Paint (Duncan Enterprises) ***Dual Brush-Pen Markers (Tombow) in the following colors: #850, #851, and #991

1. First prepare the box by painting the top of the lid white, using a stamping sponge. While still wet, blend some lavender paint around the edge of the oval as shown. Let dry. Paint the remainder of the box lavender with another sponge. When dry, sponge lavender around the edges of the lid. Let dry completely.

2. Stamp the angel on the lid using black pigment ink, emboss using clear embossing powder, and heat

from above. Color the angel, as desired, using watercolor brush markers. Highlight the angel's robe where desired, using a white, fine-point correction pen.

3. Stamp the star along the bottom edge of the box as shown with clear embossing ink and emboss in silver. Continue stamping and embossing stars until the entire box bottom is complete.

NOTE: BRUSH AWAY ANY EMBOSSING POWDER THAT CLINGS OUTSIDE OF THE STAMPED IMAGE WITH A FINE, DRY PAINTBRUSH BEFORE MELTING THE POWDER.

ENSEMBLES

Parties and gift-giving occasions are natural opportunities to show off your stamping skills! From baby showers to Halloween parties, it is easy to include rubber stamping along with the festivities by creating invitations, place cards, thank you notes, gift wrap, and much, much more. It is fun to begin with a theme and carry it through to all of the aspects of the party.

Stamps were chosen around a balloon theme for the birthday party ensemble shown. Other smaller, festive stamp images, such as the star cluster and swirl, were added to give the ensemble a feeling of gaiety and to balance the larger balloon images. Because the style of this ensemble was definitely non-formal, the type for the words and phrases were chosen carefully to reinforce this feeling. Finally, a cupcake image was added to continue the theme of a child's party. Using a single color palette throughout each piece of the ensemble also helped to reinforce its visual unity. To carry this theme through even further, balloons can also be stamped before they are blown up, using a permanent dye ink.

These attractive stamped and layered boxes and gift bags can be used over and over again!

GIFT BOXES, RIBBONS, AND BAGS

White or natural gift boxes can be dressed up for any occasion with a brayer and a few rubber stamps. Stamp matching tissue paper to coordinate with elegant gift bags that have been stamped and embossed, or stamp a large individual image on separate card stock, cut it out, and attach it to a gift bag over layers of decorative paper. Paper gift wrapping ribbons can also be stamped and embossed. Just follow the suggestions listed at the beginning of this chapter to determine which ink applications to use on your specific paper surface. Experiment to find which ones work best for you!

Chapter 6

Preserving Your Memories

With a minimal investment in supplies, you can add "scrap-booking," "journaling," or "memory-making" to your growing repertoire of rubber stamping applications! In this arena, rubber-stamped images can be carefully orchestrated to tell a story. This can be accomplished by simply surrounding a single photo with carefully-chosen rubber-stamped images that reinforce the sentiment behind the subject(s) in the photo. More complex projects can also be created using multiple techniques and images that visually encapsulate an entire event. Memory album covers, scrapbook pages, picture frames, and keepsake chests can all be embellished with rubber stamps, too. Stamping borders, frames, and backgrounds, or creating a theme collage using many of the stamping techniques taught in previous chapters, can add unity as well as make interesting visual statements.

ORGANIZE YOUR APPROACH

Begin with a theme. To avoid becoming overwhelmed, tackle only one page or theme at a time! Sort your photos into topics by subject, year, or season. You can create entire books on just one theme, such as birthday parties, school days, or summer vacations, or you may choose to create each page separately and combine all of the pages into an album that is arranged according to dates. The key here is to think creatively!

With memory pages, you are trying to tell a story, convey a mood, and provoke a memory. Photographs will need to be your central focus. Because photo pages usually revolve around a theme, the thousands of stamp images available will provide you with an unlimited amount of possibilities! Sometimes the most unlikely combinations of images can also be the most striking.

ELEMENTS OF DESIGN

Scale plays a major role in creating interesting and fun-to-view album pages. Objects which are usually very small (or large) in comparison to the subjects in the photos have the unique opportunity to be visually represented in proportions not normally observed in real life. For example, a memory page of a child's birthday party can be filled with images of balloons, sweets, or even gift boxes that look positively enormous next to the children in the photos. Or a group of friends could come out of teacups, flowerpots, or baskets. What fun it would be to place a photo of a child opening a gift box coming out of one!

Sometimes, an object appearing in a photo can even be echoed with a stamped image of a similar or related object. Rubber stamp images can also be incorporated with shapes used to display or set off your photos. For example, photos cut in the shape of hearts or mounted on paper cut into hearts would coordinate well with a colored-in background repeat of different-sized hearts.

An excellent application of a colorful random repeated background used to frame a memorable photo.

Let your stamp images give you inspiration. Different leaves stamped in autumn colors would provide an attractive background for a back-to-school page. Try masking and repeating a row of bubble stamps across the bottom of a page to help bring back the memories of your baby's—or pet's—bath-time! Just think about all of those stacks of photos taken at Christmas or other holidays—what a great use for all of those holiday stamps you might already have!

What a quick and easy way of adding humor to a single photo!

Memory-making Supplies

The two main concerns when choosing supplies for memory making are: Will they be long-lasting and are they archival and non-reactive with the photos?

The most important thing to remember in creating your keepsake albums is to make sure your photos do not make direct contact with anything that isn't photo-safe. Using archival-quality paper that is both lignin- and acid-free, along with photo-safe plastic sheet protectors, will ensure that your memories will last a lifetime.

Because acid damages photos, papers that have a low pH are too acidic to use for scrapbooks and albums. Acid-free papers are manufactured in an alkaline environment. A central component in creating acid-free paper is the use of calcium carbonate, an alkaline mineral which resembles marble dust. Besides their photo-safe quality, papers created with calcium carbonate are also brighter, whiter, and hold a cleaner image when stamped on.

Another important factor in choosing non-reactive paper is whether the paper contains lignin, a binding agent used in creating paper. Lignin is an organic substance that acts as a binder for cellulose fibers in wood and certain plants, adding strength and stiffness to the cell walls. However, lignin reacts with light and/or heat to produce chemicals and acids which will cause paper to become brittle, discolor, and deteriorate over time; therefore the best papers to use for the long-term are of archival quality, which are lignin-free and have a neutral or high pH, making them acid-free.

In addition to the correct paper, use only acid-free inks and mount your photos using glues or mounting adhesives that are acid-free. Pigment inks that are allowed to dry or are embossed are generally preferable over dye inks, which tend to fade over time and bleed if they ever get damp. Color in stamped designs with water-resistant pigment ink markers, artist-quality colored pencils, or with sponged and embossed pigment ink that has been heat-set, embossed, or allowed to dry for 24 hours or more. Because dye-based markers tend to fade when exposed to a lot of light, you should only use them with memory projects that will stay in relatively low-light conditions. Make sure that all pens and markers are acid-free and permanent.

Examples of different applications on the same theme. The memory page on the left has had a background stamped in hearts, along with the sentiment "I love you." The photos were cut out in heart shapes and layered on a contrasting paper layer also cut into heart shapes with decorative-edges. The example on the right, however, illustrates a simple collage technique with cut-out stamped letters and angled paper layers.

Embossing adds an elegant note to any memory album page. Embossing powders are pH-neutral, so they are technically acid-free. To be on the safe side, however, keep the surface of your photos from making direct contact with embossed images. The easiest way to do this is to use photo-safe plastic protective sleeves on each album page. When choosing powder colors, avoid using metallic gold or copper, which tend to age, meaning the images you emboss in these two colors today will lose their luster and change color (from gold to green and copper to brown) 3 to 4 years from now!

NOTE: Always emboss before adding photos to a page to avoid exposing the photos to any heat! Also, test your paper to make sure it will not warp permanently from the heat.

Things to avoid:
- Acidic, low-pH paper
- Inks, glues, etc. that are not acid-free
- Heat
- Humidity
- Bright light
- Washable, non-permanent markers or pens
- Glitter

CREATING YOUR MEMORY PAGES
Framing Photos

There are many different ways you can frame your photographs to highlight them on the memory album page.

● Above: One quick and easy way to decorate a photo is to create a frame using a specially-designed frame stamp. An added advantage to this technique is that you can just stamp all of your images on separate paper instead of directly onto your album page.
● Left: Use a border stamp to stamp the four sides of the frame. Align your images squarely with a stamp positioner (see page 31).

● Right: Sometimes it is desirable to draw attention to a single photo. One way to accomplish this is to frame a single photo on a page using the cut edge technique described on page 24. Use several decorative-edged layers in progressive sizes and contrasting colors. Position the layers and/or photos at interesting angles to create a more charming look. Add more interest by stamping a subtle background pattern on one of the layers.

● Right: Stamp an unusual frame using the techniques found on page 24 (Edges: Stamped Cut-outs). This time, however, cut out the center of the frame along the image outline.

● Below: Stamp individual images on paper or card stock, color as desired, and cut them out. Glue the images in a frame around the photo to create a whimsical look.

● Above right: Create a border around your whole memory page (by stamping a single image repeatedly) to frame the entire creation. Another way of creating an instant frame on an entire page is to mask the center of the page before decorating or attaching photos. Stamp a random repeat on the remaining exposed page, then stamp contrasting images or sponge color in the center masked area. Add colored patterns with a brayer or sponge. Or you can simply roll out a frame using roller stamps or different brayer techniques.

● Below right: Any large "container" image commonly used in mortise masking can become a potential frame for your photos. This clever use of stamped images combined with cut-out photo shapes will turn your album pages into works of art!

BALLOON PHOTO PAGE

MATERIALS

Outline balloon and star cluster rubber
   stamps*
Black pigment ink
Scrap book page or sheet of archival paper
Watercolor Brush Markers**
Clear embossing powder (optional)
Photo
Heat tool (optional), ruler, pencil, scissors,
   acid-free glue or tape

Used in this project: *#Y008 Party Balloons (Stampendous, Inc.) and
#A398 Stars and Circles (Hero Arts Rubber Stamps, Inc.) **Dual Brush-
Pen Markers (Tombow) in the following colors: #025, #055, #173, #195,
#371, #373, #476, #885, and #925

1. Place your photo in the center of the scrapbook
page or archival paper. Measure your photo and add
1/4" to these dimensions. Lightly mark the dimensions on the paper with a pencil and draw in guidelines with a ruler. Set the photo aside.

2. Stamp your first balloon image, positioning the
image slightly toward the center of the page and
overlapping the guideline(s). Emboss if desired.

3. Continue stamping balloons until they frame the
area. Stamp star clusters where desired. Let the ink
dry if not embossed. Carefully cut along the balloons
and portions of the guidelines with an X-acto knife.
Use a ruler to cut out the straight sections. Erase the
guidelines and color as desired.

4. Place your photo behind the frame. Glue or tape
in place.

Decorative Corners

Create corners using these different methods:

● Right: The easiest way to create mounting corners is to use either a specially-designed corner stamp or by stamping two border images at right angles to each other. These corners can be stamped on a separate sheet of paper and glued onto the photo or stamped directly onto the album page or cover.

● Left: Measure your photo and stamp corners directly onto the memory page. Cut slits and slip your photos inside.

● Below: To create unusual mounting corners, think squares! First, stamp an overall repeat design on a separate piece of paper using a textured background stamp. Cut out 1" squares from this stamped paper. Cut your squares in half along the diagonal to create triangular corners and glue onto your photos.

• Right: Attach a single stamped image over the photo or frame corners. Use foam tape for a simple 3-D effect. Or mask corner clusters of images on a separate piece of paper. Create four identical clusters for each photo. Cut them out and attach them to the corners of the photo.

• Right: Frame stamps can sometimes be too small or in the wrong proportion for your photos. Stamp the frame image once or twice on a separate sheet of card stock. Cut the image out and then cut it into quarters. Create instant expandable corners by cutting each quarter across the diagonal into a triangular corner. Draw a line along the long edges with a marker or embossing pen to complete.

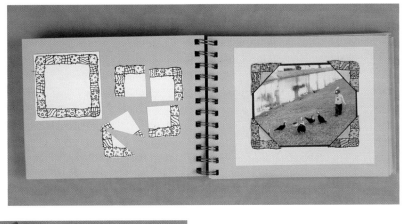

Cut-out Photos

Photos can also be cut and trimmed in creative ways:

• Cut the edges of your photo with decorative-edge scissors. Place these photos over corresponding decorative-edged paper shapes.

• Cut out specific images from the photo and use these images in a collage of photos and stamping techniques.

• Using a template as your cutting guide, cut your photos into ovals, stars, or other interesting shapes.

MORE MEMORY IDEAS

These additional tips and techniques will add a little pizzazz to your pages!

● Create a great background for your photos with an overall repeat, or create a scene using techniques such as multiple image masking, repeat design, sponging and stenciling, or shadow and movement.

● Add phrases using rubber-stamped thought bubbles or speech balloon images, or draw your own using embossing pens or pigment markers. Cut these out and glue where desired.

● Add extra interest to your page and help record special events with multiple-item collages. Include ticket stubs, map or brochure fragments, dried flowers, scraps of fabric… the list is endless!

● A simple way to invoke an element of curiosity to a single photo is by randomly gluing or stamping a couple of single cut-out stamped images to the photo page.

● Remember to incorporate colors on your page to help tie everything together!

Both of these highly-imaginative album pages utilize many of the techniques suggested above. Notice how the rubber-stamped images blend in so well with the subjects in the photos!

"FRIENDLY" TEA PARTY

MATERIALS

Large teacup or other similar container
image rubber stamp and coordinating
images of your choice*
Watercolor brush markers**
Archival dye or pigment ink
One sheet of white archival paper
One sheet of archival paper in the color of
your choice or a memory album page
Assorted photos
Scissors, acid-free glue stick

Used in this project: *#Q0006 China Tea Cup, #N036 Flowered Banner
(Stampendous), and #A1423C Holly Patch (Rubber Stampede) **Dual
Brush-Pen Markers (Tombow) in the following colors: #062, #158, #200,
#373, #603, #623, and #723

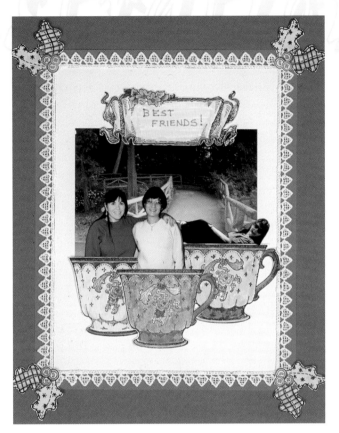

1. Cut out the central figures from your photos.

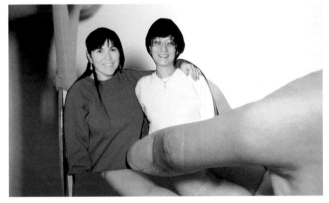

2. Stamp large teacup images on separate archival
paper stock. Emboss and color in if desired.
Carefully cut out these stamped images.

3. Arrange the stamped images on your colored
sheet of paper or memory album page. Add a background scenery photo for added interest if desired.
Position the cut-out photo images so they appear to
be coming out of the teacups and glue everything in
place. Add extra layers and images if desired.

MEMORY ALBUM COVERS

Creating memory pages offers some of the most imaginative uses for your stamps. When you combine several of these many techniques, you will create some of the most unusual memory pages you have ever seen! Of course, now you will probably want to decorate your album covers! Memory album, scrapbook, and journal covers can be decorated with any of the techniques used to decorate your photo pages. The cover design should reflect the entire contents of the album, however, instead of illustrating only one specific photo or event as its pages would do. Also, keep in mind that any photos you might choose to incorporate into a cover might be unprotected.

PICTURE FRAMES

Because they can be found in a variety of materials, frames offer many opportunities to use a multitude of stamping techniques. Frames can be square, rectangular, or oval. Some square or rectangular frames may also contain oval center openings. Don't limit their use to photos only. Wall boxes, or shadowboxes, which are deeper than most frames and come with a permanent back, can be used to display items such as medals, ribbons, other collections of small items, and special memorabilia.

Ready-to-finish wood frames that have a flat surface are easy to decorate with rubber stamps. Follow the same steps for stamping on wooden frames as you would any piece of wood (see page 119). You can also create frames with other materials. Try using leather and fabric, plus collage techniques—just tap into your imagination! Pre-cut mat boards, which are used to frame a picture within a frame, make a perfect surface to decorate, especially if you cannot decorate your outer frame. Uncut mat boards also make very convenient mounting boards. Simply attach your special memorabilia paper (or stamp project) directly to a colorful, decorated mat board and place it into a frame. Just make sure that the mat boards you are using are of archival quality!

The panda album was decorated with a simple overall repeat stamped on the entire natural kraft paper cover. The panda images were stamped on separate card stock and then cut out and attached, using the paper toling technique outlined on page 95. The extra paper layers add to the drama of this album cover. The blue album uses a photo as the identifying image for the contents of this album. A colorful brayered paper layer acts as a frame for the photo. Four decorative corners were stamped directly on the album cover and embossed in gold and subtle color highlights were added using different colored glitter glues.

SUN SWIRLS PICTURE FRAME

MATERIALS

Solid image swirl foam or rubber stamp*
Outdoor patio paint or decorative stamping paint
  in two contrasting (light and dark) colors**
Unfinished wood frame***
Scrap paper
Stamping sponges, two foam plates

Used in this project: *#61024 Primitive Sun (Rubber Stampede)
**#65019 Ivory Decorative Stamping Paint (Rubber Stampede) and
#DCP17 Golden Honey Outdoor Patio Paint (Deco Art) ***#8586
Rectangle Frame, 12-1/2" x 11" with a 3-1/2" x 5" opening (Walnut
Hollow)

1. Lightly sand any rough spots off of the wood, if
necessary. Gently wipe off any sawdust.

2. Squeeze paint on the foam plates. Apply one to
two coats of light-colored paint to the front of the
frame, using a stamping sponge. Let dry. Apply the
darker paint color onto the edges. Let dry
completely.

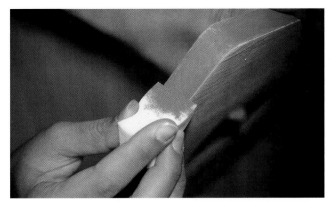

3. Apply the darker paint color to the stamp, again
using the stamping sponge. Test the image first on

scrap paper. When satisfied, stamp the image onto
the wood frame.

4. Continue reloading paint on the stamp and
stamping the image across in a repeat to create a
row. Stamp the other rows, staggering the image a bit
as shown.

Memorabilia collections do not have to be confined to album pages. Many people keep photos or other treasures in a keepsake chest or memory box. When storing your photos in such a box, make sure all of the materials used to line the box are acid-free. To prevent photos from coming in contact with items that are not photo-safe, do not keep photos in the same box as other keepsake items unless the photos are enclosed in protective sleeves.

The elegant deep blue and gold keepsake box was deceivingly simple to execute! The primed box was simply stamped repeatedly with the large swirl stamp, stamping off the edge where necessary. The oval papier mâché box features a variety of cut-out stamped and embossed photo frames that have been attached to the pre-painted surface. Extra photos were cut and attached to the center of the frames to give a glimpse of what may be inside.

Chapter 7

Embossing...
Beyond the Basics

Much of the toned-down color on the castle album cover is from the use of clear embossing powder over subtle pigment ink colors. Note how the tone-one-tone embossed stencil tile resembles embossed leather. The fanciful "shoe statement" enlists the aid of both opaque white and metallic embossing powders on a high-contrast black surface. Another wonderful effect to delight the eye is the glittery shimmer of clear rainbow sparkle embossing powder, as shown in the rose frame card.

Embossing is one of the most loved of all stamping techniques. While adding instant elegance, embossing also provides an element of mystery to stamping. There is always a bit of excitement and anticipation right before the powder melts and changes an ordinary flat image into an exquisite three-dimensional statement! The solid, raised image even acts as a resist, making coloring easier.

Embossing can be the piéce de résistance for many rubber-stamped creations. Simply put, embossed images are unequivocally impressive, especially to the uninitiated. The ease with which embossing can be done belies its unique and attractive appearance.

Follow these helpful tips for successful embossing:

● Embossed images are soft to the touch—and hot—immediately after melting. Always allow a few seconds for "cool-down" time before touching your embossed image.

● Hold your project at an angle to check the way light reflects against the embossed image. Areas that do not reflect light, or appear dull, may not be completely melted and will need to be reheated.

● To double-check that you have embossed the entire image, sprinkle embossing powder again on the cooled-down image. If the powder sticks anywhere on the image, heat again!

● Store your embossing powders in small, wide plastic containers (the ones made for sandwiches are ideal). Keep a small plastic spoon inside or taped to the lid for applying the powder to the stamped image. When finished, just tap the excess powder directly back into the container.

● A small hair paintbrush will gently brush away any excess powder that might cling to the project surface outside of the image area. Or try using a cotton swab dipped in isopropyl alcohol for more stubborn bits that cling. Do not rub the excess powder with your finger; it may mark the surface.

● For the most predictable results, stamp your image in the same color pigment ink as the opaque embossing powder you will be using.

● The temperature of a heat gun can melt paint! Be careful that the tabletop or surface the project rests on can withstand the high temperature. Surfaces such as melamine countertops or vinyl table coverings will scorch or melt with the intense heat of the heat tool. Also, make sure the actual project surface you emboss can withstand direct sustained heat of approximately 300°F.

● The heat source should never make direct contact with the project! When using a heat gun, make sure the tip is at least 2" from the project's surface. Also, never place a project inside of a toaster or toaster oven to melt the powder!

When using a heat gun, most people prefer to direct the heat at the image from above the surface. Holding the heat tool within visual range makes it easier to judge the distance between the heat source and the project, but according to embossing powder manufacturers' recommendations, the correct way to emboss on paper or card stock is to apply heat from underneath. That way, the paper heats and evenly melts the powder. This heating technique removes moisture from the paper and gives a more controlled melt.   This is especially crucial when embossing on glossy-coated paper. Because the ink stays on the surface of the coating instead of soaking into the paper fibers, the ink stays wet longer. By extending the heating time to accommodate this, the glossy paper can warp and scorch from just a few extra seconds of concentrated heat directed at its surface. Heating from underneath eliminates this problem. However, if a paper stock is particularly thick and some of the image does not completely melt when heated from underneath, a quick touch-up can be done from the top.

Embossing can also be done on other solid, flat surfaces, including leather, wood, or fabric that will not be washed. Make sure to follow the guidelines in Chapters 9 and 10 regarding correct ink use and heating procedures for these surfaces. When stamping on surfaces such as wood, leather, or fabric, heating must be done from the top.

Embossing powders and slow-drying ink must be correctly used together to create the embossed image. Among the most popular embossing combinations are clear glossy or sparkle embossing powders over opaque pigment ink. The equally favored opaque metallic or primary-colored powders are usually used over clear embossing ink or opaque pigment ink. Although some stampers never venture beyond the standard colors, there are many other intriguing powders and combinations to be discovered which positively guarantee very unusual results!

TONE-ON-TONE

For an elegant yet delicate effect, try using opaque embossing powder that matches the color of the paper. For example, stamp snowflakes on white or translucent vellum paper and emboss in white, or stamp and emboss black paw prints on black paper, as in the Lair-ed Tiger Project (see page 57). You can also match the ink color to the paper and emboss with a clear powder instead.

TRANSLUCENT PEARLS

Pearl powders are translucent powders that leave a shimmer of pearlescent color. The color tint will vary a bit, depending on what color ink these powders are applied over. For example, blue pearl has a pewter-like quality when used over black ink, but when applied over magenta or red, it has a lilac cast, and over turquoise, it appears to be blue. This powder also leaves a very subtle tint when used over clear embossing ink.

Examples of some of the more unusual embossing powder colors. Observe the varied surface textures, ranging from glittery to pearlized. Also, note how radically different one of the less opaque embossing powder looks when used on assorted colored inks. Part of the fun in rubber stamping and embossing is in experimenting with all of the possible combinations and effects! (From left to right): the opaque colors: Cranberry Glitter, Purple Metallic, Enamelware, Verdigris; the translucent colors: Plum Pearl, Black Rainbow Glitter, Peacock Glitter over clear embossing ink, Peacock Glitter over black ink (all by Stampendous, Inc.).

Examples of translucent pearl embossing powders over different color inks. From top left: Pearl Gold over clear embossing ink, Pearl Red over clear embossing ink, Pearl Blue powder over black ink, Pearl Blue powder over Metallic Blue ink, and Pearl Gold powder over Metallic Gold ink.

PEARL ROSE CARD

MATERIALS

Background/texture print and floral outline image rubber stamps*
Metallic pink pigment ink**
Black pigment ink pad
Blue pearl and plum pearl embossing powders
Rose colored pencil
5" x 7" mauve note card
3-1/2" x 4-1/4" piece of burgundy or a similar dark-colored coordinating card stock
Ivory or a similar light-colored card stock
Heat tool, decorative-edge scissors, glue stick, double-sided foam tape

Used in this project: *#A1657F Dream Garden Rose Vase and #A915E Scattered Roses (Rubber Stampede) **Encore!
Ultimate Metallic Pink pigment ink (Tsukineko, Inc.)

1. Using the pink ink, stamp the background print on the mauve note card in a random repeat pattern, stamping off the edge where necessary. Emboss with the plum pearl powder.

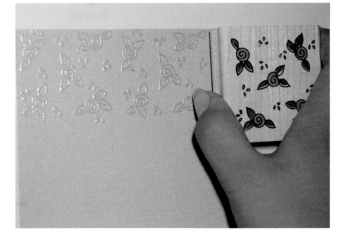

2. Stamp the floral image in black on the ivory card stock. Emboss in blue pearl. Add some soft rose shading around the image with the colored pencil.

3. Using decorative-edge scissors, cut the stamped floral image out into a 3-1/8" x 4" rectangle. Glue this rectangle onto the burgundy rectangle. Attach small pieces of foam tape behind this layered piece and attach it to the stamped mauve note card at an angle as shown.

MIXTURES

Embossing powders also come in different kinds of mixtures. There are clear, opaque, and metallic powders containing glitter to add a definite sparkle to your stamped image. Other available mixtures combine several opaque colors together that result in a faux finish effect when embossed.

As with many embossing powders, the color impact changes depending on the color surface they are placed on. Notice how the same two powder colors, Enamelware and Verdigris, seem to magically change color when used on different paper colors.

This contemporary recipe box has different sized swirls stamped on it, using different colored inks and coordinating glitter and metallic embossing powders. Because some of these powders are translucent, it is important to do a test sheet (example shown) before stamping so that the idiosyncrasies of these powders be discovered. Stamp off the edge where necessary (as described on page 20).

FLUORESCENTS

When used over clear or opaque ink on a white or lightly-colored surface, fluorescent powders have minimal impact; they actually appear to be pastel in value. Applied over dark or deeply-colored surfaces, however, their effects are extremely dramatic—the bright neon color literally leaps off a deep black or midnight blue surface!

The ultimate in personalized back-to-school supplies, the eye-popping colors on the folder or frame can be varied according to personal taste! Stamp and emboss only one image at a time, using clear embossing ink and a different color embossing powder for each image. After sprinkling the powder over the wet image, shake off the excess directly back into the bottle; this will help avoid inadvertently mixing the powder colors.

BUTTERFLY BOARD

MATERIALS

Lace edge and large and small solid image butterfly
    foam or rubber stamps*
Clear embossing ink pad
Several fluorescent embossing powders
Dark-colored acrylic paint of your choice**
Old decorative wood cutting board
Heat tool, foam brush, small fine-tipped paintbrush

Used in this project: *#53277 Butterflies Decorator Blocks (Plaid Enterprises), #A-1011 Battenburg Arc (Maine Street Stamps), and #J043 Bold Butterfly (Stampendous, Inc.) **OC158 Deep Lavender: Aleene's Premium-Coat Acrylic Paint (Duncan Enterprises)

NOTE: THIS PROJECT IS TO BE USED FOR DECORATIVE PURPOSES ONLY!

1. Paint the entire cutting board with the acrylic paint. Let dry thoroughly.

2. Stamp and emboss the lace edge along the edges of the board, alternating embossing powder colors as you go. Mask and stamp off the edge for the last image.

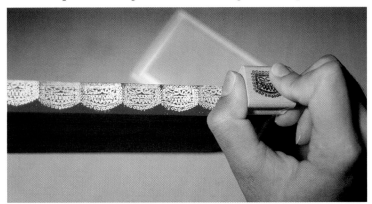

3. Stamp a large butterfly on the face of the cutting board. Sprinkle one color of embossing powder on only a portion of the image. Tap off the excess, being careful not to let the powder slide over the remaining inked image. Sprinkle one or more additional embossing powder colors, one at a time, onto the rest of the image. Heat from above to melt the powder.

4. Continue to stamp and emboss both large and small multi-colored butterflies over the entire cutting board, stamping off the edges where necessary.

83

FLOCKING AND PUFFY POWDERS

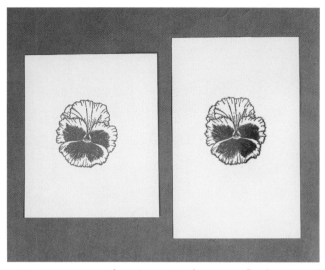

Two newer embossing powders are flocking and puffy powders. Each requires a slightly different heating process.

Flocking powder uses a two-step process. A special adhesive powder is first applied to clear embossing ink and then lightly heated from beneath until it just begins to melt and turns clear. The flocking powder is then added to the tacky image and heated a second time to completely seal and emboss. When melted properly, the flocking powder will feel fuzzy to the touch. This is a fun powder to use on solid animal images. You can also add the "fuzzy" feeling to a stamped outline image with a clear embossing marker (see Embossing Pens and Markers , page 86).

Puffy powder can be used on many surfaces, including fabric. It is applied directly over pigment, fabric, or clear embossing ink. This powder will "puff up" three to five times the original image size when heated from underneath. It is flexible and machine-washable and -dryable, as well. (Remember to use fabric ink when applying puffy powder to fabric.) Try stamping solid images in clear ink and sprinkle with white puffy powder. After the image has been heated, puffed, and dried, color over the solid image with markers.

FOILING

Stamping foils are bright, metallic-colored foils that come in sheets or rolls. There are three methods used to apply foils to an image. In the first method, the foil adheres to a stamped image, by using the same special adhesive embossing powder used above in the flock-

ing technique. This powder must be heated to become sticky. The second technique uses a special liquid foiling adhesive that is applied directly over a dried stamped image. The third method involves pressure embossing with a stylus directly on the foil. Always place the foil onto the stamped image colored side up for the first two methods.

Method 1: Embossed Foiling

Bright metallic colors can be added to a rubber-stamped image that has been stamped in clear embossing ink.

1. Stamp your image using clear embossing ink. The same special adhesive embossing powder that is used in the flocking powder is sprinkled over the image and lightly heated until it melts, turning clear and sticky. While the image is still tacky, a sheet of foil is pressed onto the warm outline. (Note: This step must be done within 90 seconds of heating.)

2. Rub the image area with your finger and then peel off the sheet. The foil sticks to the tacky surface and gives you an unusual metallic outline. Allow the image to harden (about 2 hours), or speed up the curing process by carefully heating from beneath for just a few seconds.

Method 2: Adhesive Foiling

If you choose not to emboss, the foil can be applied to a special liquid foiling adhesive that has dried overnight (it remains tacky). You can apply this adhesive to the center portions of an outline stamp. Press foils of varying colors onto different portions of the image for a unique effect!

Project designed by Deb Parks

Method 3: Pressure Embossing on Foil

Elegant three-dimensional images can be created by pressure embossing on metallic foils sold specifically for this technique.

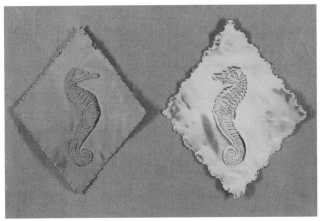

Foiling effects by Deb Parks

1. Cut a piece of foil slightly larger than the image area. Stamp on the backside of the foil with fabric ink.
2. Place the foil over a cutting mat or other thick, flat surface. Applying light pressure, trace over the image outline with a stylus or a dull knitting needle tip.

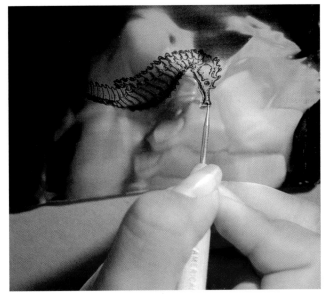

3. Gently rub away the ink with a soft towel. Apply a contrasting color of acrylic or gel stain paint over the image. While it is still wet, rub off the excess so that the paint only remains in the recessed areas.

EMBOSSING PENS AND MARKERS

All of these interesting embossing powders and techniques are not limited to stamped images alone! Embossing pens or markers come in a variety of different tip styles, including fine, medium, wide, and calligraphy. Enhance a stamped project by coloring in images with brilliantly-hued embossing markers and embossing with clear powders, or color your image with a clear embossing pen and emboss in any of the opaque or metallic colors. Try writing messages, embossing cut or torn edges, adding embossed details or background patterns, or even touching up an imperfectly-stamped and -embossed image!

> **TIP:** EMBOSSING MARKERS DRY QUICKER THAN THE INK PADS USED FOR EMBOSSING, SO YOU WILL NEED TO USE THE MARKERS AND IMMEDIATELY EMBOSS, COMPLETING ONLY SMALL SECTIONS AT A TIME.

This charming invitation boasts several added details thanks to an embossing marker! The handwritten invite was easy to execute with a calligraphy-tipped burgundy embossing marker. Both the cut edge and pattern drawn

around the edge of the black note card incorporated a clear embossing marker and gold metallic embossing powder.

STAINED GLASS LOOK

Stamped and embossed images can take on the appearance of stained glass when clear embossing powder is added to a stamped and colored image. One method is to invert a clear embossing ink pad and sponge the embossing ink directly from the pad onto an entire image that has been colored with marker. Sprinkle clear embossing powder over the image. When heated, the texture will resemble that of textured stained glass.

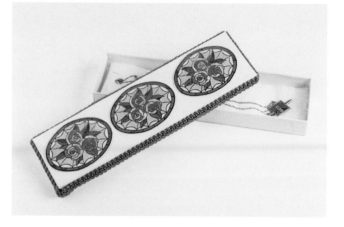

Another technique involves coloring in small areas of a stamped image with different colored embossing pens, sprinkling clear powder over them, and then heating to melt the powder. Complete the step of coloring and embossing in one section of the image at a time. The final piece will have a smooth finish.

DOUBLE OR SUPER EMBOSSING

This process creates a rich, lacquer-like finish on projects. You can use several coats of regular clear embossing powder or only one or two coats of special thick embossing enamel. Embossing enamel is a heavier granulated embossing powder specially designed for this technique.

SUPER-EMBOSSED BROOCH

MATERIALS

Outline rubber stamp in the image of your choice*
Black pigment ink pad
Clear embossing ink pad
Clear embossing powder and embossing enamel (optional)
Watercolor brush markers**
Scrap of white non-coated card stock
Piece of black card stock larger than the image that will be stamped and embossed
Jewelry pinback
Heat tool, masking tape, scissors, heavy mat or wood board, hot glue gun or permanent adhesive

Used in this project: *#G1045 Country Angel (Hero Arts Rubber Stamps, Inc.) **Dual Brush-Pen Markers (Tombow) in the following colors: #N25, #N81, #062, #243, #533, #553, #653, #761 #800, and #946

1. Stamp, using the black pigment ink, and emboss your image on the scrap of card stock. Color the image with markers, if desired. Cut out the image.

2. Using hot glue or permanent adhesive, mount the image onto a piece of black card stock. Let the glue or adhesive dry completely. Tape the backing material to the heavy mat or wood board.

3. Hold a clear embossing ink pad upside down and press it onto the entire image, making sure that it is well-inked.

4. Sprinkle embossing powder or enamel onto the inked image. Tap off the excess powder and heat from above. (Note: Keep your surface flat and level. The embossing enamel or powder will slip when liquefied). **Immediately** add more embossing powder, quickly tap off the excess, and heat again, melting the newly-added powder. (Note: It is important to completely melt each layer of powder to ensure a smooth texture.)

NOTE: If using regular clear embossing powder, you will need to repeat Step 4 until you have achieved the desired thickness. (The surface should appear smooth and even, without pits or ripples.)

5. Remove the super-embossed image from the mounting board. Trim off the excess backing paper along the sides. Glue a pinback to the back of the image.

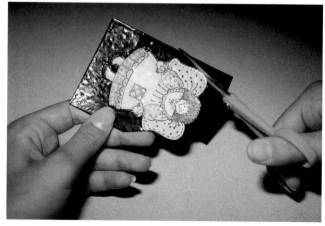

Chapter 8

Exciting 3-D Effects

If you have ever seen an Omnimax movie or one that required special 3-D glasses, you know how different—and totally amazing—that movie experience was! In the same way that a normal two-dimensional, flat movie experience was translated into a three-dimensional adventure, rubber stamping can also be transformed into a 3-D work of art with easy-to-master techniques.

With the exception of collage, all of these 3-D techniques work best with images that have distinct outlines and are easy to cut out.

3-D PLAYFUL KITTEN CARD

MATERIALS

Leaves and cat outline image
    rubber stamps*
Black dye ink pad
Watercolor brush markers**
White matte note card
Scrap of white card stock
Double-sided adhesive foam
    tape*** or pre-cut foam circles,
    scissors

Used in this project: *#B133 Ash Leaf, #J911 Cat Reaching (Red Hot Rubber!, Inc.), #B-1300 Oak Leaf, and #B-1306 Maple Leaf (Maine Street Stamps) **Dual Brush-Pen Markers (Tombow) in the following colors: #055, #173, #821, #837, #912, #925, #933, #985, and #990 ***Pop-Dots (All Night Media, Inc.)

1. Stamp the background leaves and the cat onto the note card. Color and embellish, if desired.

2. Stamp a few leaf images onto the scrap of card stock. Color the images and carefully cut them out.

3. Attach the cut-out images to the background using a small piece of foam tape or a pre-cut circle (on the back of each image). If the images are larger than those shown, use more than one small piece of foam or a pre-cut circle to secure each image so that they are completely "popped" off of the card.

QUICK AND EASY 3-D

This is a favorite technique for children and adults alike. It is also a clever way for disguising an imperfect imprint! Cut small pieces or use pre-cut circles of double-sided adhesive foam tape to raise your image off of the project's surface.

DIE-CUT BUNNY CARD

MATERIALS

Bunny image rubber stamp*
Black dye ink pad
White matte note card
Watercolor brush markers**
Fine-tipped scissors or an X-acto knife, cutting mat
Optional: matching note card, glue stick

Used in this project: *#A1314F Betsy Bunny (Rubber Stampede) and #B1119 Carrot (Maine Street Stamps) **Dual Brush-Pen Markers (Tombow) in the following colors :#062, #173, #491, #533, #553, #723, #796, #800, #933, #990, and #991

DIE-CUTS

With this technique you can create a 3-D image that magically pops up from a folded edge. The image(s) you choose should have a well-defined outline.

1. Position a folded card so the fold is horizontal. Open the card and lay it flat on your stamping surface.

2. Stamp your image so that part of the image appears above the fold.

3. Beginning and ending at the fold line, cut around the image outline on the upper portion of the card, using a sharp X-acto knife on a cutting mat or scissors.

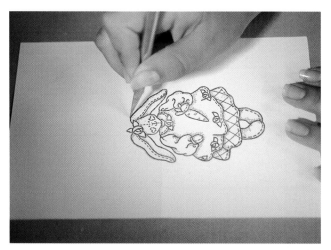

4. Bend the card on the fold and gently push the cut image area so it "pops" out. Color and embellish as desired.

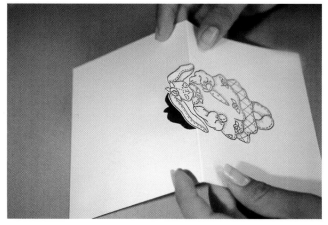

5. Optional: Because there is now a hole in the bottom portion of your card, you can either glue a corresponding piece of card stock onto the front and back of that portion of the note card or you can attach additional stamped and cut-out shapes over the cut area.

NOTE FOR ALL 3-D TECHNIQUES: For safety, children should use the appropriate style scissors instead of an X-acto knife for cutting out images.

SPRING GREETINGS POP-UP CARD

POP-UPS

A surprise 3-D effect appears when you open this card up! Position your creation either horizontally or vertically. The secret to success with this technique lies in careful measurements in Step 4 and correct placement of the cut-out image onto the center slot in Step 5.

MATERIALS

Bunny image, greeting, and assorted floral outline
    rubber stamps*
Black dye ink pad
Watercolor brush markers**
Two identical white matte note cards
Scrap of white card stock (that matches the note cards)
Glue stick, scissors, ruler, pencil, X-acto knife

Used in this project: *#345E Butterfly, #476 Tulips, #344E Flutter of Butterflies (All Night Media, Inc.), #F334 Happy Easter, #H941 Garden Bunny, #A742 Monarch Butterfly (Hero Arts Rubber Stamps, Inc.), #C4048 Eyelet Butterfly (Maine Street Stamps), and #CN018 Sweet Violet, #CN005 Clover (Stampendous, Inc.) **Dual Brush-Pen Markers (Tombow) in the following colors: #N89,#025, #055, #173, #195, #533, #553, #703, #800, #970, and #985

1. Choose two folded note cards (A and B) that are exactly the same size. Stamp and color a floral scene on the outside of card A as shown.

2. Stamp and color another floral scene on the inside of card B as shown.

3. Stamp the "pop-up" bunny image on a scrap of matching card stock. Color the bunny and cut it out. Measure the height of the image and lightly mark its center with a pencil.

4. Center the bunny image on card B, with the center mark over the fold. Lightly mark the bunny's height dimensions onto card B (both top and bottom). Remove the bunny. Create a center slot by cutting two parallel slits on card B, about 1/4" apart and matching the height of the marks. The center slot should be evenly spaced above and below the fold.

5. Gently pull the center slot out so it "pops" forward.

6. Position the cut image onto the bottom portion of the slot, *making sure the card will still fold down.* Glue in place.

7. Place card B inside of card A and glue them together.

FLORAL PLAQUE

PAPER TOLING

The ultimate in 3-D effects, this popular technique is an adaptation of a crafting art form that has been around for quite a while. The essence of paper toling is in utilizing portions of the identical image in successive layers to create the illusion of dimension. Many of these sections are bent or curved to create a realistic sense of depth. Traditional paper toling is accomplished using several, often expensive, printed copies of a drawing or painting. With rubber stamping, however, it is quite simple—and very inexpensive— to create multiples of an image or images!

MATERIALS

Small butterfly outline stamp and either a large floral outline stamp with a bow or a large floral outline stamp and a small bow stamp*
Black pigment ink pad
Clear embossing powder
Light yellow and lavender acrylic paint**
Watercolor brush markers***
White matte card stock
Unfinished oval wood plaque or plate with a raised frame or an oval wood frame glued onto a flat wood plaque****
Double-sided foam adhesive tape, low-melt hot glue gun, scissors, paint brush

Used in this project: *#C4048 Eyelet Butterfly and #K-220 Lily of the Valley (Maine Street Stamps) **Medium Lavender and Light Yellow Aleene's Premium-Coat Acrylic Paint (Duncan Enterprises) *** Dual Brush-Pen Markers (Tombow) in the following colors: #061, #243, #272, #533, #723, #813, #823, and #991 ****#3564 Oval Tray, 8" x 10" (Walnut Hollow)

1. Paint the plaque with the lavender in the center and the light yellow around the raised rim. Let the paint dry completely.

2. Stamp and emboss a butterfly on the frame. Continue stamping butterflies around the entire contour of the frame, changing the angle of the stamp slightly with each image.

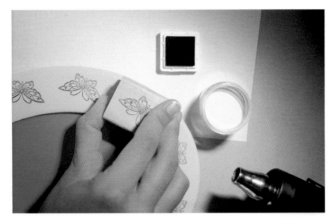

3. Stamp and emboss two floral images (and bows if needed) onto the card stock. Carefully cut out the images and color them identically with markers. Use a lavender marker to color any background area remaining around the flowers so that there is no white paper visible.

4. Cut a few 1/4" pieces of foam tape. Use the tape pieces to attach one of the floral images (and a bow) to the center of the plaque.

5. Cut out the ribbon bow and sections of flowers from the remaining stamped image(s). Gently curve the bow around your finger to shape it and give it dimension.

6. Attach the cut-out bow to the bow on the first image using hot glue in the center of the bow. Secure the outer edges of the bow in place with small pieces of foam tape.

7. Arrange the flower sections as desired over the original image, in the same place over its corresponding piece or as desired, and secure in place using hot glue in the centers and small pieces of foam tape to create a 3-D effect.

3-D Dioramas

Dioramas are three-dimensional miniature scenes partially contained within a small object such as a basket or an open box which allows the scene to be viewed from the front (and sometimes the other sides). As illustrated in this photo, it is easy to see how this technique can be extremely creative and fun to execute! It can also be categorized as a three-dimensional collage, because often other items such as containers, rocks, beads, or bits of dried floral items can easily be incorporated into your presentation.

Right: Two pieces of scrap wood molding were glued together and painted to form the base for this creative bookend. A snowflake background stamp was stamped in clear ink and embossed in white on the vertical portion of the wood to create the illusion of a winter night sky. The white painted base was given a light coating of varnish. While still wet, a fine prisma glitter was sprinkled over the base. Stamped images that had been masked to create a scene were cut out and hot glued onto the sparkly base after it was dry. Additional cut-out images were then added and glued on in successive rows.

In-the-Round

The purpose of this unusual technique is to create projects which can be viewed partially or completely from different or all sides. To best accomplish projects in-the-round, choose only bilateral images. To determine whether an image would be suitable, first stamp it on scrap paper and cut it out. Draw a line down the center of the image and fold it in half. If the right and left side match up exactly (or nearly so), the image would be perfect to use to create miniature sculptures in-the-round.

This striking miniature sculpture was created using three different bilateral images. The vase uses the identical construction as the ornament project demonstration on the next page, but instead of a cord, a green toothpick has been inserted to serve as a stem for the multi-layered paper-toled sunflower. Delicately balanced, a two-layer butterfly perches on the petals of the flower, carefully anchored in place with hot glue.

IN-THE-ROUND CHRISTMAS ORNAMENT

MATERIALS

Bilateral ornament image rubber stamp*
Clear embossing or gold pigment ink pad
Gold embossing powder
Watercolor brush markers**
Two white note cards
Scissors, heat tool, low-melt hot glue gun, 4"
  piece of gold cord

Used in this project: *#A1047H Star Flake Ornament (Rubber Stampede)
**Dual Brush-Pen Markers (Tombow) in the following colors: ##346,
#565, #856, and #985

1. Stamp and emboss three ornament images on the note card. Carefully cut them out and color each image identically.

2. Gently curve each ornament image in half so the centers bend back.

3. Place the three images right side down. Fold the cord in a loop and tie it at the ends. Lay the knotted end against the top of the first image and glue in place. Apply glue along the right curved edge of the first image. Quickly attach the second image to the first, matching up sides.

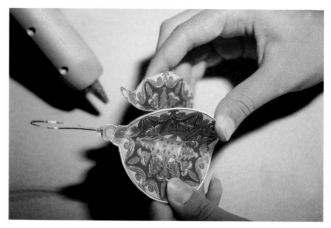

4. Repeat for the second and third images. Glue the remaining image sides (first and third) together.

Trompe L'oeil

A painting technique used by the ancient Romans, trompe l'oeil, which literally means "to fool the eye," is a very quick and clever way to create the illusion of dimension. By simply adding a shadow with a light- to medium-gray watercolor brush marker or a colored pencil along one side and the bottom of an image, the image now magically appears to be jumping off the page!

This whimsical card is a breeze to make! Stamp the images as shown, using different ink pad colors. Color in the pencils with watercolor brush markers, using the blending and shading method described on page 38. Draw a fine black line to connect the letter "Y" with the pencil image, along with a pretend cut line from the edge of the card to the dog's foot. The finishing touch, however, is the simple gray "shadow" drawn in along one side of each object, using a medium gray marker. Don't forget to stamp an envelope to match!

Casting Shadows

Another way to create a very dramatic and realistic dimensional effect to your rubber-stamped creations is to draw in cast shadows. This is actually a fine arts technique used in realistic drawing and painting that has been adapted to use with rubber-stamped images.

In real life, shadows appear as a result of light striking against a solid three-dimensional object which will not allow the light to pass through it and illuminate the area behind the object. Therefore, the first thing you will need to do after stamping your images is to decide where you want your light source to be in relationship to the stamped objects. After you have made that decision you can determine where the shadows will be cast. For example, if the imagined light source is in front of the object, the shadow cast should be behind the object, but if the light source is behind the object, the shadow will need to be drawn in front of the object. The lower the light source is in relation to the base of the object the longer the shadow will be. Conversely, light sources from above the object cast relatively small shadows. The results are all up to your imagination!

COLLAGE

Creating a visual relationship with unrelated items can be a stimulating challenge! Combinations based on "difference" is the key to this technique. Collage is simply the layering of various items with dissimilar textures, dimensions, and styles, all from surprisingly diverse sources. These items can be as simple as layers of various-colored and -textured papers or as complex as combining paper with wood, leather, cork, buttons, feathers, ribbons, wire, or other items. All of these contrasting pieces are then glued together onto a common surface to create a unity out of disharmony.

A dimensional technique for all levels of ability, collage makes use of bits and scraps of almost anything. Because everyone approaches collage a little differently, this technique is certainly one of the most individual ways of expression. A single stamp image or an unusual item might trigger the idea for a collage. Often, the collage just develops as more things are added to it.

In the graphic arts, the most dynamic designs are based on contrasts. When approaching collage, you must consider shape, texture, and color. Shapes should vary in size, angle placement, and type. Take advantage of the many textural possibilities of paper.

Projects at left and below designed by Deb Parks

Torn paper has a different feeling than cut paper shapes. Handmade papers, or those crumpled or crimped, can add unique textural interest to your collage. Color contrasts can be as severe as black against white or a gradual progressive layering of colors, such as green + yellow + orange + red.

COLLAGE TIPS:

● Some types or brands of glue may discolor or warp paper, while others may not have the holding power for heavy items. Test to see which glue works the best for your application before using it on the finished project. Different glues include: rubber cement, thick white craft glue, glue sticks, liquid glue, hot glue, and double-sided tape or foam tape.

● If the project starts to warp from the glue, place a heavy book over it for several hours. Protect any surfaces from extra glue seepage with a layer of wax paper or plastic wrap.

● Save little bits and scraps of papers, ribbons, single-stamped or embossed images, and other interesting items for future collage projects.

Project designed by Karen Johnson for All Night Media

• Decorative punches are perfect to use for collage! Punch stars, hearts, and other shapes from scraps of paper-backed patterned metallic or holographic wrapping paper. Glue these small confetti shapes onto your collage. Or, use the larger punched-out scraps of paper as part of your project.

• Hand-torn edges are the rage for collage! An easy way to create a more controlled torn edge is to paint a line on your paper with a fine wet paintbrush and then tear gently along the wet line for a soft, feathered edge.

• Stamp phrases across several layers of paper using sets of alphabet stamps. Better still, combine several styles of type in the same work!

• Collage is not limited to two-dimensional paper surfaces only. Try creating collages on items such as papier mâché boxes, gift bags, or even on album covers or wooden frames.

EMBELLISHMENTS FOR ADDED 3-D FUN

The following is just a partial list of the possible materials you can use to further embellish your rubber stamped creations. This list seems to grow daily as designers continue to discover new ways to incorporate rubber stamps into every segment of the craft industry and beyond!

• Glitter glue paints sparkly translucent color onto stamped images. Note: This is a very slow-drying glue.

• A quicker way to add sparkle is with glitter and a quick-drying glue pen. Applied over a colored image, the clear "prisma" glitter will magically—and unexpectedly—change the original color of the image.

• Confetti shapes come ready-made in different metallic shapes. Or, create your own shapes from paper using any number of decorative shape punches.

• Crimped paper adds textural interest to many projects. Use a special tube wringer or crimping tool to create different colored strips or simply cut a piece of corrugated cardboard, discarding the outer layer of paper.

• Dimensional fabric paints can be used to outline large stamp images which are either stamped, appliquéd, or decoupaged onto surfaces such as fabric or wood. They can also add dimensional details, such as tendrils on vines, bubbles in a sea life scene, or snow on a tree.

• Puffy paint raises up when heated. If it is wet when heated, the paint will assume a rather puffed-up, rough texture. A smoother, more controlled texture can be achieved, however, if it dries before it is heated.

• Buttons, ribbons, lace, ribbon roses, small jewels, and other easy-to-find craft items can add a special touch to many rubber-stamped projects. Just use your imagination!

• Brayer an interesting background. Cut shapes out of it and use them in combinations with other 3-D techniques and embellishments.

• Glue small wiggle eyes onto animal or people images for a touch of humor!

Chapter 9
Fabric and Leather Stamping

Stamping on fabric and leather are unique opportunities to further develop your stamping skills. As you will soon discover, these surfaces are much different than paper. You will need, therefore, to develop the special skills and knowledge necessary to successfully stamp on them.

STAMPING ON FABRIC

Fabric stamping is a fun way to show off your rubber stamping skills. The range of fabrics you can choose to stamp on offers quite a variety of interesting applications and looks, from the soft country appeal of tea-dyed muslin to the contemporary glitz of acetate. As you have already seen in previous chapters, much of the discoveries in rubber stamping are the result of creative experimentation, and the same holds true with fabric.

TYPES OF FABRICS

Fabric preference is personal, but when choosing fabrics to stamp on, you will need to pay close attention to the weave and surface texture. The tighter the weave and smoother the texture, the clearer the stamped image will be.

Different weave fabrics will yield different results. Here's a simple test: Use a piece of tightly-woven cotton or cotton/polyester blend fabric and a piece of knit cotton or cotton/polyester blend (such as a T-shirt is made of). Press a clean, dry rubber stamp onto both of these surfaces. When you remove the stamp, notice that you can still see the impression in the knit fabric. This very softness and buoyancy, intrinsic in

the knit material, also creates a potential problem; because the stamp actually sinks into the fabric, you are more apt to get a back-print unless the stamp has been carefully trimmed.

When stamping on fabric, take extra care to ink *only* the *image area* of the stamp, especially when working on knits or thicker fabrics. Trim your stamps if necessary to reduce back-print. When at all possible, purchase a small piece of fabric, similar to the type you will be stamping on, in order to practice stamping your images.

It is important to wash and dry your fabric before stamping to remove any sizing and allow for shrinkage. Smooth out any wrinkles with an iron on a non-steam setting, prior to beginning your project. One-hundred percent natural fibers feel softer to the skin, but the addition of polyester will resist wrinkling. To prevent bleeding, make sure the fabric is completely dry before stamping or coloring on it.

TEXTILE INKS AND PAINTS

Textile, or fabric, inks and paints can easily bleed through a single layer of fabric. Because they are permanent, you will need to protect the stamping surface and/or the rest of the garment. To prevent paint and ink from bleeding through to other fabric layers or your work surface, place a protective sheet of wax paper-covered cardboard directly beneath the fabric layer you are stamping on. (Corrugated cardboard is not suitable because the ridges can create an uneven stamping surface.) Flat, pre-made fabric boards are ideal to use with garments such as T-shirts because they provide the perfect shape and surface to place garments onto while stamping. Make sure the fabric is taut and lying flat against the board. Use masking tape to secure sleeves and other loose parts to the back of the board.

Depending on the look you want and the type of stamps you are working with, you can use either fabric paint, glazes, or ink. Some stamps will work better with paints and glazes, while others are best with ink. This determination becomes even more important when different fabric surfaces and contents come into play.

Fabric inks are available under a variety of labels. They come in ready-made stamp pads and feel similar to pigment ink when stamped with. They also come in bottles with special tops made to dab the ink onto the stamp. You can even purchase non-inked pads and create your own color combinations using ink from re-inking bottles.

Some fabric ink formulas are non-toxic, non-irritating, and safe for children to use. Other fabric inks, and some textile paints, however, contain irritants or are labeled toxic. These products usually contain solvents and are permanent without heat setting. Use caution when selecting fabric inks or paints, especially when stamping with children or those people who are chemically-sensitive! Read labels carefully to see which specifically state they are nontoxic, non-irritating, and safe for children.

The non-toxic fabric inks available today are vibrant and easy-to-use. They must, however, be heat-set with an iron to become permanent. To heat-set ink, use a non-steam setting; the time and temperature will depend on the contents of the fabric you are using. A pressing cloth is recommended for all heat settings. Hold the iron on the press cloth/stamped fabric as long as you can without scorching the fabric. Use the appropriate temperature setting for the fabric as per the instructions on the label. Constant heat application is preferred over interrupted heating (lifting the iron on and off several times). In addition to heat setting, refrain from washing the newly-stamped fabric for one week to help ensure its permanence. Washing a stamped garment in cold water will help prevent ink colors fading.

Fabric paints and glazes are permanent without needing heat setting. Fabric paint is thicker than ink and the stamped results will look more opaque with less of the fabric weave showing. Fabric glazes are more translucent than the opaque fabric paints and are adversely affected by brightly-colored or dark surfaces, which distort the glaze's color. Translucent glazes can be used to create a looser, less-defined look. Because it is almost impossible to completely remove unwanted paint from fabric, glazes offer a way to cover up unwanted back-prints and still create a fantastic project by simply stamping, painting, or sponging over these areas. The paint or glaze needs to be first squeezed out onto a separate palette surface like disposable plastic or foam plates or trays. (Note: Paper plates are not suitable. The paint tends to dry out quickly and unevenly on this surface.) The paint is then applied directly to the foam or rubber surface of the stamp, using a sponge, sponge brush, or brayer.

It is easy to correct incompletely stamped images; simply touch up "missed" spots with paint and a fine-tipped paintbrush, or carefully correct ink images with the fine-tipped end of the matching textile marker.

Need a wider range of colors to choose from? There are special textile mediums specifically designed by paint manufacturers that will turn acrylic paints into suitable mediums to use when stamping on fabric. Remember to follow the manufacturers' directions when creating these mixtures.

Fabric ink, paint, and acrylic paint dry quickly and will ruin your stamps if not cleaned properly and promptly. While you are working on a project, place your dirty stamps, rubber side down, on a tray or plate of damp paper towels. This will help keep the paint or ink damp until you can clean your stamps. If the paint or ink does dry onto a stamp, however, use a specially-formulated paintbrush cleaner, such as The Masters, to clean your stamp. This non-toxic product is safe to use on rubber and will dissolve dried-on paint in a matter of minutes.

It is always wise to test your stamp images and the

ink or paint method out on a sample of fabric first. Even if you are stamping on a finished garment or fabric item, you can usually purchase 1/4 yard of a similar fabric at a fabric store to practice on. Check the garment label so you can match the fabric contents. If you are sewing your own items, stamp and cut pieces first before sewing them together. It is easier to stamp on the flat, seamless fabric. Plus, if you make a stamping "miscalculation," you can always just cut out a new piece and restamp it!

STAMPS FOR FABRIC STAMPING

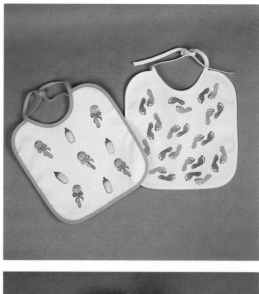

Solid image stamps are ideal to use on fabric. These images are available in either a rubber die or a pre-cut foam die. They are also available in sets of scored foam images that each represent a portion of a complete image. Scored foam images are specially designed to work with translucent glazes.

It is also possible to use many outline images. When choosing images to stamp with on fabric, look for the bolder outlines without fine detail. The lines of a softer, more delicate stamp image may not all show up clearly on fabric. Deeply-etched outline stamps with some or little detail tend to have a cleaner outline with ink, while the more solid images most often work best with paint or glazes.

Images that follow the above formulas, however, might take a different turn, when the variable of fabric surface is added. The trick to knowing whether ink or paint is best suited for your particular application is to practice on fabric similar to what you'll be using for your project.

PAINT APPLICATION

The way in which you actually apply paint to a stamp–and the tool you use–will determine the effect of the stamped image. Experiment with the following techniques to discover which look(s) you prefer:

● Using a foam brush or stamping sponge, apply the paint by stroking it several times in one direction only.
● Stroke the paint on side to side. Then re-apply the paint from top to bottom.
● Apply the paint with a circular motion.
● Lightly dab or stipple the paint onto the stamp image until the entire surface is covered. Do not over-coat the stamp by applying too much paint to it!
● Create a rainbow palette on your plate or tray. Squeeze three colors onto your plate. (Make sure to avoid using the following combinations in the same rainbow: blue/orange, red/green, or yellow/purple. These complementary colors will turn muddy if used next to each other.) Apply this rainbow to your stamp with a stamping sponge, foam brush, or brayer. Make sure you pick up and apply the paint in one direction only!
● Color different parts of your image with different colors. For example, apply red paint to an apple, green paint to the leaf, and brown paint to the stem. Work quickly, however, so the paint doesn't dry!
● You can also blend and shade colors on a stamp to give the image an interesting, more realistic, look.

It is rather difficult to apply paint directly to an outline stamp image with a brush. You can, however, create a paint "stamp pad." Simply squeeze your paint onto a foam plate or tray. Using a foam brush, spread the paint out in a thin, even layer, about two to three times the size of the largest stamp image. Let the paint cure for a minute or two. Press your stamp into this "pad," tapping it once or twice into the paint, and stamp directly onto the fabric. Repeat the steps, adding more paint as needed.

WELCOME BANNER

MATERIALS

Solid image rubber or foam alphabet, leaf, scroll, or other images of your choice*
Green, golden yellow, purple, and burgundy stamping paint**
1 yard light-weight interfacing
1/2 yard cotton batting
1 yard cotton/polyester fabric plus a scrap for testing
3/8" thick dowel (18" long)
1/2 yard corded trim
22" x 28" piece of wax paper-lined poster board
Foam plates, stamping sponges, scrap paper, scissors, tailor's chalk or pencil, sewing machine or needle and
thread, scrap paper (18" long), dye ink pad (any color)

Used in this project: *#63003 Primitive Set, #64007 Alphabet Set, and #61023 Decorative Scroll stamp from the Decorative Stamping series
**Decorative Stamping Paint (Rubber Stampede) in the following colors: Straw #J457J207, Sweetheart Blush #J127J097, Seminole Green #A352A228, and Eggplant #G284H017

1. Create the pattern piece, following the instructions on the next page. From the pattern, cut out two pieces of fabric and one piece of batting. Stamp the letters on a piece of scrap paper, using the dye ink. Let dry. Place the top layer of banner fabric over the stamped paper. Lightly mark the letter positions on the fabric with tailor's chalk or a pencil. Place the top banner fabric over wax paper-lined poster board.

2. Squeeze the burgundy and purple paint onto a foam plate. Apply the burgundy paint to the "W" stamp with a sponge, using a gentle dabbing motion. Apply the purple paint randomly over the burgundy. When the stamp is evenly covered with paint, do a test imprint on the fabric scrap. If you are satisfied with the result, reapply the two paint colors and stamp onto the banner. Continue with the rest of the letters, always testing each stamp imprint first, until the word "WELCOME" has been printed out.

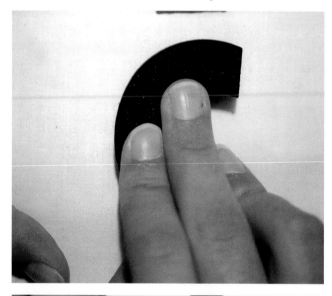

3. Stamp the scroll in golden yellow as shown, followed by the leaves. Let all of the paint dry.

4. Place the unstamped fabric piece on top of the stamped piece, right sides together. Place the batting piece beneath these two pieces. Machine- or hand-sew around all of the sides, leaving the top edge open. Turn the banner right side out. Fold the top edge inside and pin in place. Topstitch all around the banner, 1/8" from the edge. Fold the top edge back to form a casing around the dowel. Pin in place. Remove the dowel and stitch the casing in place along the pinned edge. Place the dowel back into the stitched casing. Tie the cord trim onto the dowel's ends to hang.

TIP: CLEAN THE INK OFF OF THE ALPHABET STAMPS BEFORE APPLYING PAINT.

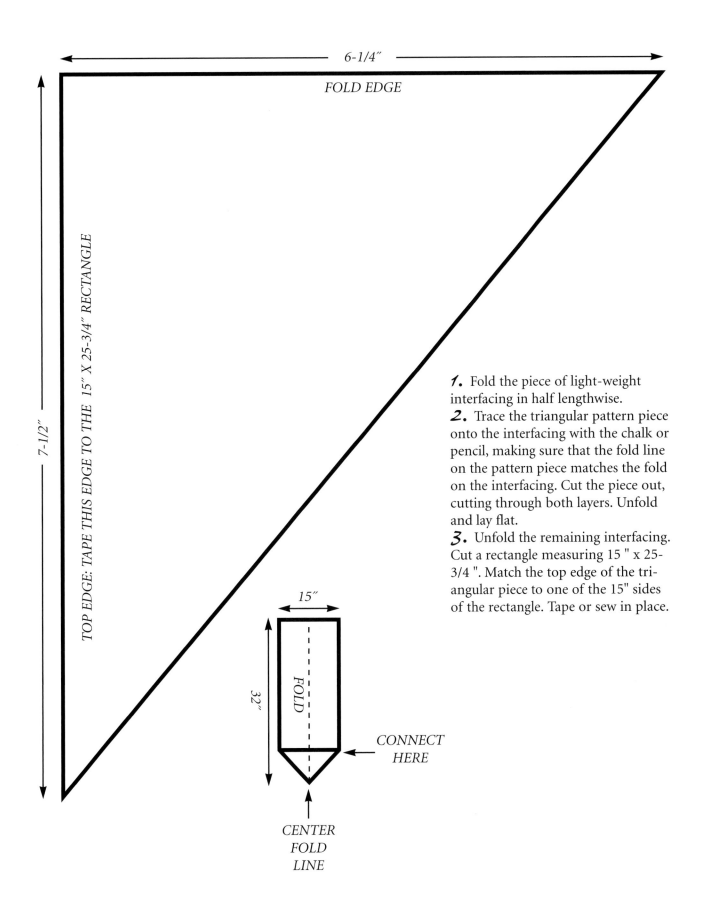

6-1/4"

FOLD EDGE

7-1/2"

TOP EDGE: TAPE THIS EDGE TO THE 15" X 25-3/4" RECTANGLE

15"

FOLD

32"

CONNECT HERE

CENTER FOLD LINE

1. Fold the piece of light-weight interfacing in half lengthwise.
2. Trace the triangular pattern piece onto the interfacing with the chalk or pencil, making sure that the fold line on the pattern piece matches the fold on the interfacing. Cut the piece out, cutting through both layers. Unfold and lay flat.
3. Unfold the remaining interfacing. Cut a rectangle measuring 15 " x 25-3/4 ". Match the top edge of the triangular piece to one of the 15" sides of the rectangle. Tape or sew in place.

RAINBOW HEART T-SHIRT

MATERIALS

Solid heart, zigzag, and scroll foam or rubber stamps*
Purple, lavender, green, mauve, medium blue, yellow and golden yellow stamping paint**
A cotton or cotton/polyester blend T-shirt (pre-washed, dried, and ironed, if necessary)
Scrap fabric
Foam brushes or stamping sponges, foam plates, T-shirt board, masking tape

Used in this project: *#63003 Primitive Set, #61023 Decorative Scroll, and #61002 Heart from the Decorative Stamping series (Rubber Stampede)
**Decorative Stamping Paint (Rubber Stampede) in these colors: Straw #J457J207, Lavender #68622, Kelly Green #J132J097, Dusty Mauve #J779K116, Denim Blue #I644J017, Yellow #68638, and Eggplant #G284H017

1. Wash and dry your T-shirt. Place it onto a shirt board and tape the arms in place onto the backside of the board.

2. Squeeze purple paint onto a foam plate. Apply the paint to the zigzag stamp and practice stamping and repeating a straight row on scrap fabric. When ready, stamp the zigzag pattern across the center of the shirt.

3. Squeeze lavender, blue, and mauve in a row onto another foam plate. Using a foam brush or stamping sponge, load the applicator by wiping it in one direction and picking up all three colors.

4. Apply paint to the heart stamp as follows: Wipe the sponge down the right half of the heart. Rotate the sponge so that the paint color that appears in the center of the heart will now be on the right side of the sponge. Wipe the sponge down the left half of the heart.

5. Stamp the heart image on the T-shirt in the center above the zigzag row to create the top row of hearts first. Repeat the lavender, blue, and mauve rainbow combination again on the far right and left sides of the top row, and then twice again below the

zigzag row in a staggered position for the bottom row of hearts. Wash the stamp. Continue by stamping the hearts with a kelly green, yellow, and golden yellow rainbow combination.

6. Repeat Steps 3 to 5 with kelly green, yellow, and golden yellow, stamping two hearts in the empty spaces on the top row and three hearts in the center and right and left sides of the bottom row.

7. Complete the T-shirt by stamping lavender scrolls across, below the bottom, and above the top rows of hearts.

COLORING IN YOUR IMAGES

Textile markers are permanent markers designed to color on fabrics. They are quite easy to use and are a good choice for adult-supervised children's fabric projects. A special colorless blending marker even makes realistic color blending and shading possible. However, like some of the fabric inks, some textile markers may also need to be heat-set to become permanent. Read the manufacturers' labels and follow the steps outlined on page 103 for heat setting ink.

You can also color your stamped images with fabric paint, acrylic paint, or glazes properly thinned with the correct paint medium (thin either fabric or acrylic paint with a textile medium and thin glazes with either a textile medium or clear glaze). Do not thin down the paint or glaze with water or it will bleed outside of your image outline! Apply the medium first onto the stamped image. Add a dot or two of the color(s) desired and carefully blend it into the medium with a fine-tipped brush. This technique will make your color translucent, allowing the stamped outline to remain dark and visible. For more opacity, use proportionately more paint than medium.

Some helpful guidelines for artistic shading using acrylics and textile medium on fabric include:
- Start with very little pigment mixed into the medium; gradually add more pigment if a more intense shade is desired.
- Small, semi-firm brushes are the best for working the paint onto the fabric.
- Begin with the palest colors you desire for the image, proceeding toward the darker ones.
- Shading can be added in while the paint is still wet, but you can also add shading after the base color is dry, resulting in a more dramatic contrast.
- Blending strokes may be long or short, depending on the type of fabric and the effect you wish to achieve.
- Keep a dry rag available to remove excess color from your brush or to dab away excess paint on the fabric. Remember to use a light touch.
- The more layers of color you apply, the more hidden the image's outline becomes. If details get obscured, dab it with a rag to remove some of the paint. Or, try stroking the outlines back in with a little black acrylic paint on a tiny brush.
- Avoid using black or white to make colors darker or

Example of an image stamped on fabric and colored in with textile markers. A blender pen was used to blend the colors and give the pear a more realistic appearance.

This quick and easy decorative pillow was made by stamping a lovely pansy stamp onto a ready-made cotton doily. After the black textile ink (Fabrico, by Tsukineko) was heat-set, all of the images were then colored in with permanent textile markers (Fabrico Dual Markers by Tsukineko). When the images were dry, the decorated doily was simply hand-tacked onto a ready-made 12" pillow.

lighter because these denser pigments can obscure stamped lines very easily. Instead, purchase a darker or lighter shade of acrylic paint.
- Hot, humid air might cause the fabric paint or medium to remain tacky. For consistent results, painting is best done when the air quality is not extremely hot or humid.

EMBELLISHMENTS

For added dazzle and dimension, complete your fabric-stamped project with embellishments. After the stamped image has dried, add outlines, squiggles, dots, or details with dimensional fabric paint. You can also attach jewels, ribbons, or fabric-safe glitter with fabric glue.

WINTER SCENE PILLOWCASE

NOTE: Before coloring in your images, allow the stamped image to dry completely. Depending on the fabric, temperature, and humidity, this could take anywhere from a few hours to a day or two. Use your testing fabric as a guide. It is always safer, however, to wait 24 hours before coloring the images. Outline images stamped with fabric ink can be colored in after fabric ink has been heat-set. Check manufacturers' instructions regarding heat setting inks or paints.

Project designed by Gail Green and Deb Parks

MATERIALS

Large snowflake and outline image snowman border rubber stamps (Note: Single
snowman images can be masked and
stamped to create a border instead)*
Black and ultramarine textile ink pads**
Acrylic paint, textile medium
Standard size white polyester/cotton pillowcase
Poster board, cut to fit inside the pillowcase
Scrap fabric, washable fabric trim and fabric
glue (optional), stamp positioner, tracing
paper, dye ink pad (any color), paint
brush, iron, press cloth

Used in this project: *#F865 Large Snowflake and #H099 Snowpeople
Border (Hero Arts Rubber Stamps, Inc.) **#18 Ultramarine and #82 Real
Black Fabrico Premium Multi-Purpose Craft Ink (Tsukineko)

1. Wash and dry the pillowcase. Iron out any wrinkles if necessary. Place the cut poster board inside of
the pillowcase, glossy side up.

2. Carefully check the rubber on your stamps and
trim off excess rubber to prevent back-prints.
Practice stamping your images on scrap fabric using
the textile ink.

3. Begin with the hem edge. As per instructions for
positioning images on page 31, place your tracing
paper against the positioner and stamp the snowman
trio onto the tracing paper with the dye ink. Let dry
completely. Position the stamp border 1" from the
right edge and stamp the snowmen onto the hem
edge, using black textile ink. Allow the ink to dry for
a few minutes. Repeat four times across the entire
edge.

4. Clean your stamp. Applying ink to only a portion of the stamp, stamp a snowman figure (or
whatever is needed) on both the right and left side to
complete the border. Stamp off the edge where necessary.

5. Stamp a blue snowflake in the center of the pillowcase. Complete the pillowcase by stamping snowflakes around the central one in a random pattern.

6. Heat-set all of the stamped images with a warm
iron set on a non-steam setting. Color the images in
using acrylic paint and a textile medium, following
the guidelines outlined on page 110. Glue or sew on
washable fabric trim along the pillowcase's hem edge.

STAMPING ON LEATHER

With its unmistakable charm and lasting beauty, leather is a natural surface for rubber stamp art. From belts and moccasins to jackets, leather is one of the most exotic wearable surfaces to stamp on. Other leather craft items, such as book covers, furniture, and frames, can be a stamp artist's dream come true!

The clarity of the stamped image depends on the type of leather you stamp on. You will need to stamp on the smooth side of the leather, because the softer side will not take the image as clearly. Images will appear crisp and clear on a hard, smooth leather surface, such as cowhide. The more napped surfaces of the softer, suede-like finished leather should only be stamped on with fabric paint and abstract, solid images, because inked outline images do not imprint clearly on the rougher texture.

For the best results on smooth leather, use opaque fabric inks. You can also use dye or pigment ink as well as fabric or stamping paint. Because opaque embossing powders tend to stick and smudge slightly on the leather, embossing on leather should only be done with clear embossing powder over colored opaque pigment or fabric ink.

Non-dyed leather darkens naturally when exposed

Projects on this page designed by Kari Lee for The Leather Factory

to light. If you prefer a more tinted look, you can color natural leather using an inked brayer. Dye ink rolled over leather in overlapping strokes will result in a deeply-stained effect, whereas applying pigment ink will give a smoother overall color. Try several of the brayer techniques outlined on pages 46 and 47.

If you choose to color an outline image stamped on leather, use fabric markers or "paint" onto your image with fabric inks. You can apply fabric ink directly from the ink pad onto the leather using the tip of a dried-out marker. This "ink painting" will result in a more opaque coverage, as well as the choice of more vibrant colors. When coloring your images, use acrylic paint, markers, or stencil creme. Textile markers can be used for small areas of color; when used in larger sections, they tend to streak.

It is essential that stamped leather be sealed to prevent it from absorbing dirt, oils, or water. Always heat-set inks and markers that require this step before applying the leather sealant. For a non-toxic, child-safe method, apply two to three very light coats of Fieblings Leather Stampables Sheen over the finished project. Or, if you prefer, you can spray on one or two coats of professional Leather Sheen aerosol. As an extra precaution, make sure to use this product outdoors for proper ventilation.

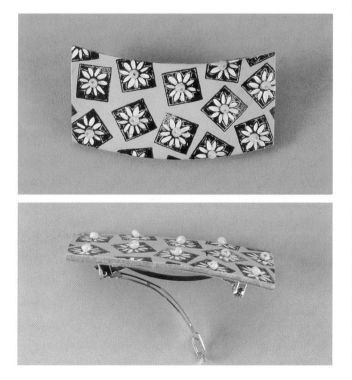

LEATHER TILE FRAME

MATERIALS

Assorted floral outline image rubber stamps*
Gray, brown, rust, and black textile ink**
Medium and dark green, orange, pink, yellow, blue, and purple permanent textile markers***
Smooth-texture natural leather pieces large enough to cut three strips, each measuring 10" x 1-1/4"****
5" x 7" piece of dark gray or black mat board
Leather sealant*****, leather glue******, X-acto knife, metal ruler, stamping sponges, heat tool, long-nose tweezers or pliers

Used in this project: *CN005 Clover, #CN018 Sweet Violet, #CN015 Primrose (Stampendous, Inc.), Sunflower and Rose from #2401R Floral Set (All Night Media), #A805B Romantic Rose (Rubber Stampede), #15-10B Tiny Daisy (Good Stamps Stamp Goods), and #C-1247 Morning Glory (Maine Street Stamps) **Fabrico Premium Multi-Purpose Craft Ink (Tsukineko) in the following colors: #81 Cool Gray, #54 Chocolate, #53 Autumn Leaf, and #82 Real Black ***Fabrico Dual Marker (Tsukineko) in the following colors: #22, Spring Green, #63 Forest, #12 Tangerine, #33 Rose Pink #11 Lemon Yellow, #19 Cerulean Blue, and #36 Wisteria ****Stampable Leather (The Leather Factory) *****Fieblings Leather Stampables Sheen (The Leather Factory) ******Aleene's Leather and Suede Glue

1. Cut three 10" strips of leather, each measuring 1-1/4" wide. Stamp the different flowers in black on the leather strips, leaving room between the flower images to cut. Let dry for a few minutes. Heat-set the ink with your heat tool, held 4" above the surface for just a few seconds. **Do not heat too long or the leather will begin to curl!**

2. Color in the flowers with textile markers as shown.

3. Cut various lengths of "tiles" to create the sides of the frame and cut various widths of tiles for the top and bottom of the frame. Fit the tiles together on the piece of mat board as shown, trimming where necessary and leaving small spaces between each tile. Fill in the larger spaces left with blank spacer strips cut out from the leather scraps.

4. When you are satisfied with the spacing, remove each tile, one at a time, and randomly sponge rust and the brown textile ink around the edges of each leather tile. Heat-set each tile. (Tip: To avoid burning your finger, hold each small leather piece with a long-nosed tweezers or pliers, while you heat set the ink.) (Option: You can also apply ink onto a stamping sponge directly from a textile marker and gently sponge color onto the leather. Use a different sponge for each color.)

5. Sponge gray ink randomly on the mat board. Heat-set the ink, using the heat tool as in Step 1. Glue the tiles to the mat board with the leather glue. Let dry. Carefully coat the entire frame with leather spray. Let dry completely.

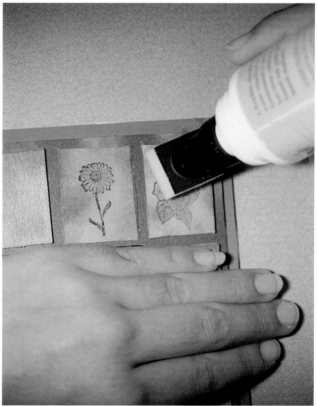

Chapter 10
Home Decorating: Inside and Out

One trip to any do-it-your-self home center reveals a myriad of new and exciting ways to decorate your home. With all of the techniques and tools currently available, rubber stamping is a natural extension of this creative arena.

Whether stamping on walls, furniture, or accent pieces, rubber stamps can enhance the ambiance of your home on a shoestring budget. With just a stamp or two, the proper paint, and the techniques that follow, you can easily give a facelift to many items, such as walls, kitchen cabinets, paneling, mirrors, or furniture like tables, chairs, and armoires. In fact, almost any flat surface that can be painted or stained can be transformed into a work of art with rubber stamps!

FAUX FINISHES

Faux finishes are painted surfaces mimicking interesting or natural textures such as wood, marble, or aged metals. Many faux finish effects can be achieved by applying two to three colors of paint onto a single surface, using a specific brush application for each layer. These effects include sponging, rag rolling, texture painting, combing, faux moiré, faux marble, and a faux granite or faux wood grain effect. The results can be subtle when similar color

It is easy to create a custom decorator look using even the most basic stamping techniques! Repeat design, one of the simplest skills to master, is used in each of the pieces represented in this photo.

values or hues are brought together or very dramatic with higher contrasting color combinations. Information on these fascinating decorating techniques are available in books, magazines, and manufacturer brochures available at craft and book stores, newsstands, and home decorating centers.

Stamped images can be very striking against a faux finish backdrop such as a wall or furniture surface. By applying colors layer by layer directly onto a stamp you can create some of the exciting faux finish effects mentioned above. The color combination and the manner in which the paint is applied to the stamp will determine the type of effect.

MATERIALS
Foam and Rubber Stamps

Although almost any rubber stamp can be used to create decorative accents for your home, a great deal of thought went into developing stamps to decorate walls and other sizable aspects of home decor. Most of the detailed outline image rubber stamps used to create greeting cards and other diminutive projects were too small and contained too much detail for stamping patterns and borders on expansive walls and other larger-scale home decorating projects like cabinets and tables. Because these stamp art projects were meant to be viewed from a distance greater than arm's length, the images needed to be clear and visible and in a larger scale. Entire lines of home decorating rubber and foam stamps, including sets with coordinating themes and images, have been developed to fill this stamping need. Similar to and often intermixed with smaller solid image stamps used for fabric stamping, these images also are more suitable in style and design to coordinate with commercial home furnishings and accessories. One advantage in the "foam-on-foam" (a foam image on a foam mount) home decorating stamps over using rubber mounted on wood or foam is the ease with which paint or glaze can be washed off the stamp with running water and a rag. Another is that the spaces between the solid image sections is spaced further apart, preventing paint from accumulating where it would cause a back-print.

You might also discover, especially because these solid images are large, that you may need to apply pressure a little differently with each stamp you are using. One stamp may need more pressure in the center so the image prints more solidly, while another might need more or less pressure on an edge or detail

This dashing light switch plate adds a contemporary flair to a neutral decorating scheme. Prepare an unfinished wood light switch plate by painting on a sponged faux-finish surface. Then, simply dab black, brown, and gray paint onto the stamp, using a foam brush or sponge, and stamp! Keep applying paint and stamping until the entire switch is covered. Make sure to stamp off the edge where necessary or as desired. To finish, seal with one or two coats of varnish for added permanence.

to print clearly. And, if you do choose to use wood-mounted rubber outline stamps, they will need to be chosen carefully. Test the image result on paper first. Outline images that contain little or no detail will work the best.

Paint, Glazes, and Ink

Most of the stamping you will do on a wall will be with stamping paint or translucent glaze. Acrylic paint can also be used, but sometimes results in a textured, rather than smooth, imprint. Ink that needs to be heat-set is not advisable to use when stamping on walls. Solvent-based permanent inks are available for home decorating. These inks give a very clear, sharp image; however, most of these inks are toxic or contain irritants. **Read labels carefully! Follow manufacturers' guidelines and use proper ventilation with an exhaust when using materials that are toxic or contain irritants. Children or adults who are chemically-sensitive should avoid using these products.**

DECORATING WALLS

Decorating walls with wallpaper and borders can be a very expensive and difficult undertaking. Just looking through the hundreds of books available to select the right prints and colors for your room can be an intimidating task for most people!

Rubber stamping your walls, however, offers another option. With just a few stamps (even just one or two), you can custom decorate your room easily and inexpensively. Plus, as a bonus, the stamps are reusable and can also be used to create accent pieces or coordinating wall coverings! You can choose from a large selection of images to fit your style and theme. And, of course, the color choice is yours!

Most wallpaper patterns are simple repeated patterns that use one or more images in rows of patterned or alternating repeats. Follow this lead when stamping on your walls. Color schemes can be as simple as one color repeated across a painted wall or more complex, involving staggered repeats and multiple colored images. Keep the patterns and colors simple when first starting out!

The key to successful wall stamping is careful planning. Plan your pattern and spacing first on paper. Stamp multiple images and cut them out. Using these cut-out images, arrange them in rows or patterns. You can also use them to make decisions on spacing.

And, as always, practice first, using the exact techniques and materials that you will be using for your finished project. Stamping on a vertical surface feels very different than stamping on the more customary horizontal surface, so before attempting to decorate your wall, practice stamping on one first. Tape a piece of paper onto a wall to practice on. The height you stamp at also makes a difference. A shorter person will feel much more comfortable stamping at a different point on the wall than a taller person. Try stamping at different heights to discover at which point you might need either a step stool or ladder, because the changing angle of your hand will affect your ability to stamp a good, clean image. Determine these factors before you begin the finished wall so there will be no surprises (or mad dashes for step stools)!

PREPARATION

First, paint all of the surfaces you wish to cover before stamping on them. (Glossy paint or varnish will make stamping difficult; stamps tend to slip around on a glossy surface). If you choose, you can faux finish the wall before stamping. While the paint is drying, plan your design or pattern on paper and practice stamping each individual image.

To stamp a patterned repeat on an entire wall, measure and lightly mark where each imprint is to occur. This can be done with a plumb line and chalk, by eye, or the methods described below for borders. You will quickly get the rhythm of the pattern as you stamp.

BORDERS

Creating a border is a quick and simple way to decorate. This device can be used on a plain painted wall, as a visual divider between colors on a wall, or in conjunction with an entire stamped wall.

1. Decide where you want your border to appear. Measuring from the ground up, lightly mark on the wall with pencil or chalk and draw a light line or place a low-tack masking tape all of the way across the wall. Continue around the entire room. This will be your guideline for lining up your stamp image. If you choose to paint your border area a different color, measure and mark a second line. Run masking tape along the top and bottom edges of the areas you wish to paint. Paint this area, and after the paint is completely dry, remove the tape, and use the line dividing the colors as your guideline.

> **NOTE:** USE MASKING TAPE LABELED LOW-TACK OR EASY RELEASE, BECAUSE THESE HAVE A GENTLER ADHESIVE THAN REGULAR MASKING TAPE AND WILL PREVENT THE TAPE FROM PULLING FLAKES OF PAINT OFF THE WALL WHEN IT IS REMOVED.

2. Apply paint to your stamp. Make a test print first on scrap paper. This will help you determine whether you have overloaded the stamp with too much paint or not applied an even coat.

3. When you are satisfied with the imprint, line up the bottom edge of the stamp against the guideline. If, however, you have carefully trimmed a special home decorating foam stamp so that you no longer have a straight edge on the stamp, use some point of the stamp to line up along the guide line edge. Or, if you need the straight edge, you can temporarily mount the stamp on a block of wood, a small gift box lid, or even cardboard, using one of the temporary mounting adhesives or glues on the market. Apply even pressure to the stamp and lift the stamp straight off the wall to remove. Let the image dry.

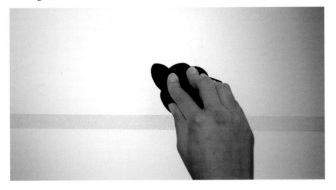

4. Create a "spacing strip" by cutting a piece of paper the width of the space desired between images. Place the spacing strip next to this first image and position your stamp again, this time aligning it with both the guideline and the spacing strip. Stamp your image. Continue in this manner until you have stamped the entire border.

If you want your images to be stamped at angles, create "angle strip" triangles out of paper, cut to match the angle you desire. The triangle should be at least as tall as the stamp is long. Line up the bottom edge of the angle strip against the guideline and position your stamp against the longest edge of the triangle. Flip the shape with each alternating image.

Once you have created an awesome look on your walls you can turn your attention to coordinating the rest of the room. You can stamp on window shades, lamp shades, curtains, furniture, linens, and even wood or concrete floors!

As demonstrated throughout this book the art of rubber stamping can go far beyond paper. In fact, it is such a versatile medium that you can stamp on almost any solid surface! All you need is a little imagination, some basic stamping skills, and guidance to know how to coordinate the proper materials to the appropriate surface.

WOOD

From antiques to unfinished furniture and craft items to garage sale finds and attic treasures, wood is available in a variety of useful pieces just waiting to be decorated. Wood has many of the same excellent qualities of paper. It provides a hard, stable surface that can easily be stamped on with all types of stamps. Wood can be embossed or stamped with stamping paint, gel, or different types of inks. Because unfinished wood is so porous, however, the surface gener-

Paint glazes give a soft, loose look to stamping. Here, an unfinished wooden table is given a cheery country flair with overlaying colors of translucent glazes.

The simple techniques used on the teddy bear shelf and decorative mini bird houses are the basic ones learned in the beginning chapters of the book. The simple stamped border embossed on the small wood chip heart box is the perfect accent for the faux-jeweled top. The secret to successful stamping on this unusual shape is to begin stamping in the inside corner of the heart and stamping off the edge when you reach the tip. Finish the second half of the box by beginning again in the inside corner and stamping in the opposite direction. Projects designed by Deb Parks: birdhouses and box.

ally needs to be sealed first before stamping it.

Make sure to check your piece first for defects or rough spots. A light sanding with a fine- to medium-grain sandpaper is desirable before sealing the wood. Depending on your taste and level of expertise, paint your wood piece using acrylic paints in a single color or in dozens of delightful color combinations. If you prefer the natural wood to show through, simply coat it lightly with a clear matte varnish. Wood can also be sealed with any of the fascinating faux finishes or gel stains now so popular.

Stamp and color on pre-sealed wood with permanent ink or paint. Unless you are embossing, however, it is best not to use ink or markers that require heat setting for permanence, because the heat from a heat gun can damage acrylic paints and many varnishes. If you choose to emboss, make sure you keep your heat source a little further away from the wood piece and keep it in constant motion to avoid causing the paint or varnish to bubble. Do not overheat or reheat the embossed image!

For extra durability, one or two coats of varnish can be brushed or sprayed over the finished piece. Use high gloss for a lacquer look and a softer satin or matte finish for a more natural appearance.

Want to jazz up a tired kitchen? Sometimes all that outdated kitchen cabinets need is a coat of paint or a faux finish followed by one simple stamp image placed in the center of each panel. In fact, you can give the same kind of facelift to old, tired wood furniture. Apply a coat of paint or paint a faux look such as wood grain or granite. Follow this with a simple repeated stamp pattern in a solid or complementary faux finish look. Or, decoupage stamped images onto dark finished or more textured wood surfaces (see page 134). In fact, when complex or exact repeat positioning is necessary, decoupage can't be beat!

It is remarkable how much the background surface color can affect the outcome of the various ink and embossing powder colors. Although the three clocks were stamped with identical images and pattern, the results are all strikingly different. Each clock was stamped in a repeat pattern, stamping off the edge where necessary to vary the pattern image, and then embossed using different colored embossing powders and inks. The top portion of each overlapping row was masked to reduce the height of the trees as they recede into the background. The ink/embossing colors used for each of the clocks are as follows: (black, top left) silver/silver, gold/gold, copper/copper, copper/clear; (antique, bottom center) silver/silver, gold/gold, copper/copper, black/clear; (ochre, top right) black/clear, chocolate/clear, autumn leaf/clear, gray/clear. All images were stamped using Fabrico Premium Multi-purpose Craft Ink (Tsukineko).

Many of the techniques demonstrated throughout this book can be performed on a wood surface. The carrots on this delightful picture frame were stamped in black in a random repeat and embossed with clear powder. They were then colored with textile markers and embossed with clear embossing powder. Note that the picture inside of the frame is also a simple stamped design.

What a difference some faux-finish sponging and decoupaged stamp images can make! Anyone's kitchen can acquire a fresh, updated custom decorator look without the expense of replacement cabinets! Simply remove the existing cabinet doors and sponge two or three colors of acrylic paint onto each of them to create the faux-finish look. (DecoArt's Patio Paint Daisy Cream #DCP15 and Antique Mum #DCP19 were used on the cabinet pictured.) If desired, sponge paint onto the remaining portion of the cabinets. Using Decorative Stamping Paint (Rubber Stampede), stamp the vegetables and the checkerboard borders onto pieces of coordinating card stock. When dry, cut out the images, position them, and apply them to the cabinet doors with a decoupage paste, such as Mod Podge (Plaid Enterprises). To finish, add a couple coats of varnish for extra durability.

OUTDOOR DECORATING

Home decorating does not need to be limited to the inside of the home only! You can also stamp outdoor projects using outdoor weather-proof and fade-resistant decorating paints. Begin your creative outdoor adventure by stamping rural mailboxes, wood decks, sheds, and planter boxes, or even concrete, bricks, and flat outdoor metal items—the sky's the limit!

Above: This child's picnic table was faded and worn from outdoor exposure, but a new coat of brightly-colored paint and the fun alphabet and stars stamped on it with the same outdoor paint make this table both durable and appealing.

Left: Stamped vines and flowers wind around this attractive and unusual rural mailbox. Outdoor paint makes this work of art impervious to the elements!

This decorative planter box has been painted and stamped for outdoor use using outdoor paint. The faux-tile look was achieved by simply painting straight lines around the three stamped images. The remainder of the planter box was then painted in the same contrasting color as the lines.

SUNFLOWER PAVING BRICKS

MATERIALS

Solid foam double sunflower and leaf (or
　other floral image) rubber stamp
　(Optional: A single sunflower image can
　also be used)*

Yellow, golden yellow, white, green, and rust
　outdoor paint**

Paving bricks (in whatever quantity necessary
　for your use)

Stamping sponges, foam plates, small paint-
　brush

Used in this project: *#64006 Decorative Stamping Spring
Garden Set (Rubber Stampede) **Patio Paints (DecoArt) in
the following colors: #Sunshine Yellow (DCP06), Sunflower
Yellow (DCP20), Sprout Green (DCP13), Patio Brick
(DCP16), and Cloud White (DCP14)

1. Wash any dirt or debris off of the paving bricks you will be stamping on. Let dry completely.

2. Squeeze outdoor paint onto the foam plates, with the two yellow hues and the white on one plate and the rust and green on another. Apply the two yellow colors to the double sunflower image, painting a different yellow on each flower. Dab white paint onto some of the petals. Carefully apply the brick color to the center of the flowers.

Note: If you are using a single flower image instead of a double, you will have to apply paint to it twice and stamp it twice on the brick in Steps 2 and 3.

3. Practice stamping the image on an extra brick. When you are satisfied, reapply paint to the stamp and quickly press it onto the top half of a paving brick. Apply even pressure over the entire stamp and then lift it straight off. Reapply paint to the stamp and stamp a second image below the first. Touch up any missed areas with the paintbrush.

4. Apply green paint to only one of the leaves on the stamp and stamp it next to one of the flowers. Repeat the same single leaf image seven times around each of the flowers, stamping off the edge where necessary.

Chapter 11

Goof-Proof Techniques for the Faint-at-Heart

Many of the techniques demonstrated throughout this book can also be used to correct or camouflage a mistake. The trick is to think of "mistakes" as "surprises," instead of fatal errors. At this point, you have probably tried many of the techniques in this book with great success; however, any problems you might have encountered with stamping a perfect image are simple to avoid, once you are aware of what causes them.

This chapter has a three-fold purpose: First to help you identify the underlying reasons for the most common stamping "mistakes." Second to offer special tricks to camouflage "mistakes." And, finally, to introduce ways to help prevent "mistakes" on those surfaces that are more difficult to stamp on.

COMMON IMPRINT PROBLEMS

1 Incomplete prints result from uneven pressure. Make sure you are stamping onto a surface that is flat and rigid. Large stamps require a different type of pressure application than do their smaller counterparts. The best way to apply even pressure to a large wood-mounted stamp is to press in different areas over the entire image with one hand, while holding the stamp firmly on the edges with the other. Pressing with a flat wood block or other object also helps distribute the pressure evenly onto the entire image.

It can be a little more difficult to get a complete clear imprint from a very finely-detailed stamp image than from one with simple outlines. This can result from either incompletely inking the stamp, using

1

uneven pressure when stamping the image, or from a poor-quality foam cushion on the actual stamp. This problem usually occurs in the central area of the stamp, although it can occur anywhere. Adding a little extra pressure, therefore, over the center or areas that seem to have the most detail should alleviate this problem.

Stamp images that are more triangular or L-shaped also present their own unique problem. Because the square or rectangular wood mount is missing a section of rubber beneath it, it is easy to pick up unwanted ink on the mount when inking the stamp and create a back-print on the project surface. This type of stamping problem created by the unequal surface hiding beneath the solid mount can be avoided by carefully holding and pressing the stamp only over the area of the mount that has a rubber image portion beneath it.

2 Poor impressions from solid image stamps are usually a result of ink or paint that partly dried before the

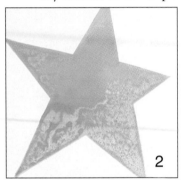

impression was stamped. To avoid this problem, use ink and paint with longer drying time.

3 Outline images that produce a back-print can easily be trimmed with a small, fine-tipped scissors. Trim away the excess rubber that is causing the problem, being careful not to knick the actual image. This includes large blank areas inside of the stamp image as well.

4 Back-prints from solid foam home decorating stamps are usually a result of paint or ink that has crept onto the sides of the image sections. Although the extra paint is not visible on the foam's surface, it can imprint on your project surface with the pressure of stamping. Before stamping, check the image side of the stamp after applying paint or ink and wipe off any extra that might have gone in between the image sections.

TRICKS FOR COVERING UP MISTAKES

You have just spent a great deal of time and energy working on a wonderful note card. And then… disappointment! The very last image did not stamp as planned. Do not despair! You have just arrived at a new creative junction. The most ingenious stamping techniques around were born out of mistakes! Instead of starting over again or giving up stamping forever, the following tips and tricks can be used to correct those unexpected surprises all stampers get from time to time. In fact, it is possible that some of these very techniques were developed by very inventive (and perhaps stubborn) stampers who refused to simply toss out a fantastic project for one imperfect image!

CUT-OUT "COVER-UPS"

The easiest techniques to use for covering up imperfect images are with cut-out "cover-up" images. Simply stamp the identical image—or one slightly larger—on the same paper stock. Color, if desired, and cut it out. Now glue the new image directly onto the project. For a 3-D effect, attach this new image right over the imperfect image with a small piece of foam tape. This cover-up image can also be stamped on sticker paper, cut out, and stuck over the bad image.

COVER UP WITH EMBELLISHMENTS

What can you do with a stamped border whose very last image is slightly askew or just doesn't connect? One easy way to disguise this mistake——oops, surprise—is with a simple ribbon bow, button, or other embellishment. No one will ever know!

> NOTE: LARGE FRAME AND "CONTAINER" IMAGES USUALLY CONTAIN LARGE BLANK RUBBER CENTERS. AFTER TRIMMING THE CENTER SECTIONS OUT, REMOUNT THE BLANK RUBBER ONTO A PIECE OF WOOD TO USE FOR THE MIRROR IMAGING TECHNIQUE IN CHAPTER 3.

SAND IT OFF

Wood can be one of the most forgiving surfaces to correct. Simply remove the imperfect image from unfinished wood with finely-grained sandpaper. If the wood has been painted, gently sand most of the image off and then repaint the wood. Most of the time, unwanted images or smudges stamped with a slow-drying ink or paint can be quickly wiped off with a damp terry cloth towel. Incomplete images stamped in paint can also be touched up with a paintbrush.

DRAW IT ON

"Skipped" areas of outline stamps can easily be corrected. If the image was stamped with pigment ink and embossed, embossing pens and clear powder work miracles! Test the embossing pen first on matching scrap paper for a good color match. Incomplete outlines of images that have been stamped with dye ink can be filled in with fine-tipped watercolor brush markers. Make sure to complete all color blending within the actual image first, however, to prevent the marker outline from bleeding into another marker color.

USE YOUR IMAGINATION!

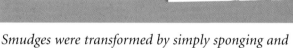

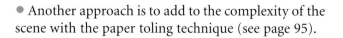

Smudges were transformed by simply sponging and stenciling

Imperfect images or ink smudges in complexly-masked scenes sometimes cannot be adequately corrected using the methods outlined above.

● One interesting solution is to cut out the entire scene with decorative scissors. Use this cut-out scene as the center point for a paper layered collage.

● Another approach is to add to the complexity of the scene with the paper toling technique (see page 95).

● Depending on the images used, embossing pens can also be used to "draw in" details, transforming ink smudges into confetti dots, squiggles, or tendrils on vines.

● You can also add to a smudge with sponging more of the color onto the project.
● Try writing a message to cover up the ink spot.

PREVENTING MISTAKES ON DIFFICULT SURFACES
Fabric Appliqué

Fabric can be one of the most difficult and unforgiving surfaces to stamp on because of its uncertain absorbency and textural irregularities, back-prints, misprints, and uneven coverage. These are all common obstacles that often present themselves when working on fabric—even with seasoned stampers. Textile ink, stamping paints, and glazes are permanent, so once they have permeated the fabric, they are almost impossible to remove completely.

Stamping on dark, brightly-colored, or rough fabrics can also present a multitude of problems. Most inks and paint just do not show up well, or sometimes not at all, on dark fabrics. Images stamped in black on bright colors such as red or turquoise can look great, but coloring in these images will most likely result in distorted or reduced colors. Rough textures like denim and burlap can cause a rather unclear and unevenly-imprinted image. Problems like these can be *very* frustrating.

One easy way of getting around all of these complications, however, is to create an appliqué. Stamping on a medium-weight white or off-white fabric will allow any color used to remain true. Closely-woven fabrics that have at least some synthetic fiber in them, including cotton/polyester blends or acetates, give the clearest images.

Silk, shiny acetate, or similar synthetic fabrics can be ideal fabrics to use when creating a garment using fabric appliqué. These fabrics are closely-woven and less porous than cottons. Detailed, outlined stamps appear very crisp on these fabrics. Just make sure you use a pressing cloth and a little lower temperature iron on them when heat setting and bonding them to the garment.

The appliqué method can also provide confidence for the faint-of-heart when attempting to stamp on an expensive or one-of-a-kind garment. By stamping on a fabric other than the finished garment virtually nothing can go wrong. There are no imperfect imprints, unwanted ink, or paint splotches with this method! You can stamp your image on the appliqué fabric as many times as you need to get a perfect image to use.

There is only one image restriction when creating an appliqué: choose an image with a very contained shape or outline that is easy to cut out. Otherwise, you will have to create your own shape, such as a heart or a patch, around the stamped image.

Stamp your image(s) with fabric ink or paint. Let the images stamped in fabric ink dry and then heat-set per the manufacturer's instructions. Color in as desired with textile markers. If the item is to be washed, attach the appliqué to your garment with an iron-on adhesive. Seal the edges if desired with fine-tipped fabric paints designed for that purpose.

For images stamped with paint, use the coloring methods described in Chapter 9. Attach the painted appliqué with an iron-on adhesive. Use a press cloth and a low temperature setting for your iron. Press a longer time with your iron to compensate. If the items are **not** going to be washed, and the surface the images are to be attached to is relatively smooth, you may prefer to use a press-on adhesive.

Interesting fabrics such as shiny acetates or metallics create unusual fabric appliqués to iron or stick onto paper projects. You can even turn solid image stamps into templates. Using a light-colored ink or paint, stamp a solid image onto the wrong side of a plaid or printed fabric that has been attached to iron-on adhesive. Cut out the outline shapes and attach them to another fabric surface. Add details to the image, if desired, with puffy paint or other embellishments.

STARRY VEST

MATERIALS

Large solid star image rubber or foam stamp*
Any light color dye ink
1/4 yard each: silver and gold metallic fabric
1/2 yard iron-on adhesive**
One denim vest (pre-washed to remove sizing)
Gold and silver fine-tipped dimensional fabric paint
Masking tape, iron, ironing board, two large disposable press
    cloths (1/2 yard of muslin is a good choice), scissors,
    shirt board

Used in this project: *#H1147 Big Solid Star (Hero Arts Rubber Stamps, Inc.) **UltraHold
HeatnBond (Therm O Web)

NOTE: METALLIC FABRIC HAS A
LOOSE WEAVE. USE TWO PRESS
CLOTHS WHEN IRONING THIS PROJECT:
ONE TO PROTECT THE IRONING BOARD
SURFACE AND ONE BETWEEN THE IRON
AND THE FABRIC BEING HEATED. CHECK
THE PRESS CLOTH FOR TRANSFERRED
ADHESIVE AFTER EACH IRONING STEP. IF
THERE IS SOME RESIDUE, REALIGN THE
PRESS CLOTH SO YOU WILL ONLY BE
IRONING ON A CLEAN AREA OF THE
PRESS CLOTH. DISCARD AFTER USE.

1. With press cloths in place and following the manufacturer's directions, fuse the metallic fabrics to the iron-on adhesive. Make sure the iron is on the low/warm setting. Leave the paper backing in place.

2. Stamp eight stars on the wrong side of the fabrics, directly on the paper backing. Let the ink dry and carefully cut out the shapes. Remove the paper backing from each star.

3. Using the photo as a guide, place the stars on both front sides of the vest. Secure each of the stars with a small (1/8") piece of masking tape. When you are satisfied with the arrangement, remove the tape from each star on one side of the vest and, following the manufacturer's directions, iron the stars onto the garment, **one at a time**, using the press cloth. Make sure the iron does not accidentally touch the masking tape on any of the other stars! Repeat these steps for the other side of the vest.

4. Place the vest on the shirt board and tape the back of the vest in place to the board. Paint along the edges of the stars with a fine-tipped fabric paint, using gold or silver, depending upon the star's color.

Appliqué Scenes

Outline stamp images offer a myriad of thematic possibilities for apparel decoration. When stamped on different colored fabric, coloring in images with textile markers or paint becomes unnecessary. Appliqué gives you the flexibility to move all of the images around until you are satisfied with their placement. The advantage to this is obvious: because the images are already in their final form, important color relationships can readily be determined.

Multiple Layer Appliqué

Another version of creating appliqués from rubber-stamped images involves piecing together multiple sections of the same image from several identical images stamped on different colored fabrics. Choose a simple, large image with clearly-defined areas for this technique.

BEAR HUGS STOCKING

MATERIALS

Outline image bear, star, and heart rubber
  stamps*
Black textile ink pad**
Green felt Christmas stocking***
1/8 yard each of yellow, red, and tan fabric
Iron-on adhesive****
Red fabric marker*****
Iron, ironing board, two large disposable
  press cloths (1/2 yard of muslin is a
  good choice), scissors

Used in this project: *##G909 Tucker Bear (Hero Arts Rubber Stamps,
Inc.), #A1317C Country Heart Patch, and #A1321C Country Star Patch
(Rubber Stampede) **#82 Real Black Fabrico Premium Multi-Purpose
Craft Ink (Tsukineko) ***Craftwares Pre-Sewn Christmas stocking
(JanLynn Corporation) ****Ultra Hold HeatnBond (Therm O Web)
*****#14 Poppy Red Fabrico Dual Marker (Tsukineko)

1. With press cloths in place and following the
manufacturer's directions, fuse the fabrics to the
iron-on adhesive. Trim off the excess iron-adhesive.
Leave the paper backing in place.

2. Using the black ink pad, stamp three bear images onto the fused tan, yellow, and red fabric pieces. Let the ink dry completely.

3. Carefully cut out the tan bears. Cut out the sweater portion only from the yellow bear images and remove the paper backing. Place the cut-out yellow sweaters over the sweater portion of the tan images and iron in place.

4. Cut the three red hearts out of the red bear images. Iron these hearts onto the yellow sweaters. Position the three bears across the stocking's folded cuff and iron in place.

5. Using the black ink pad, stamp stars onto the yellow fabric and hearts onto the red fabric. Heat-set when dry. Color the hearts on the star images with the red fabric marker.

6. Cut out all of the hearts and stars. Position these images on the stocking and iron them in place.

PIECEWORK: PATCHES AND QUILT SQUARES

This mistake-proof fabric stamping technique is similar to both appliqué and quilting. It differs from appliqué, however, in that the images stamped onto your fabric do not need to be cut out along a definite outline, nor do they need to be attached with adhesive. Instead, any stamp image can easily be utilized, including outline stamps that consist of scattered or difficult to cut out shapes.

Piecework is completed primarily on a rectangle or square of fabric, although patches with other simple outline shapes, such as a heart or star, are also fun to create. An entire scene can be created using such techniques as masking or repeat design. When completed, your hand-stamped and -colored piece can be hand- or machine-stitched onto an article of clothing or used as the center accent for a larger quilt.

> **TIP:** WHEN ATTACHING A LIGHTLY-COLORED, MORE OPEN-WEAVE FABRIC PATCH, QUILT SQUARE, OR APPLIQUÉ ONTO A DARKER COLORED FABRIC, SOME OF THE DARKER COLOR MAY SHOW THROUGH, DULLING OR DISTORTING THE COLORS OF THE PATCH, QUILT SQUARE, OR APPLIQUÉ. TO AVOID THIS PROBLEM, SIMPLY CUT AND FUSE A LAYER OF INTERFACING OR BATTING BETWEEN THE STAMPED PATCH, QUILT SQUARE, OR APPLIQUÉ AND THE FINAL SURFACE.

This pumpkin patch has an extra-thick layer of batting under it to help prevent color distortion from the dark fabric underneath. It also gives it a 3-D look.

PANDA QUILT SQUARE TOTE BAG

MATERIALS

Panda and solid leaf rubber stamps*

Black, light green, and dark green textile ink pads**

Canvas tote bag***

6" square scrap of white fabric

5-1/4" x 5-1/2" piece of green print fabric

4-1/2" x 4-3/4" piece of cotton batting

Iron-on adhesive****

Fine-tipped dimensional fabric paint*****

Flat, rigid piece of cardboard to match the inside dimensions of the tote bag

Optional: 1/2 yard decorative trim, fabric glue

Used in this project: *#K956 Panda Hugs (Red Hot Rubber!, Inc.) and #A1102E Monkey Fern (Rubber Stampede) **Fabrico Premium Multi-Purpose Craft Ink (Tsukineko) in the following colors: #21Emerald, #22 Spring Green, and #82 Real Black ***Craftwares Pre-Sewn Tote Bag (JanLynn Corporation) ****Tulip Pearl Jade Fabric Paint (Duncan Enterprises)*****Ultra Hold HeatnBond (Therm O Web)

1. Place the piece of cardboard inside of the tote bag so all of the seams are positioned beneath the board. Alternating green inks as you go, stamp the leaf images onto the tote bag in a random pattern. Heat set.

2. Stamp the panda onto the piece of white fabric. Heat set. Following the manufacturer's instructions, attach the iron-on adhesive to the back. Cut out the fused stamped panda image into a square measuring 4-1/2" x 4-3/4". Attach iron-on adhesive to the back of the batting. Remove the protective paper from both pieces. Place the panda piece over the batting and fuse the two pieces together.

3. Attach iron-on adhesive to the back of the green fabric. Center and iron it onto the bag. Position the fused panda quilt square onto the green fabric and iron in place.

4. Draw a line around the edges of the panda quilt square with the fine-tipped dimensional fabric paint. Let dry. Glue decorative trim across the top hem of the bag and around the quilt square, if desired.

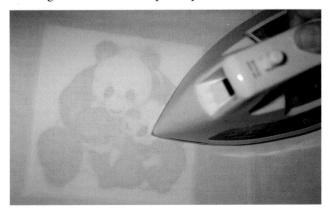

DECOUPAGE

A cousin of appliqué, decoupage is a simple technique that makes it possible to decorate non-fabric surfaces that are normally impossible to stamp. When stamp mounts simply do not fit into corners and tight inside surfaces, decoupage can offer the perfect solution! Fitting complicated patterns onto items such as a round vase or an irregularly-shaped shelf also becomes less intimidating with this method. Because the rubber stamp images are stamped on separate fabric, paper, or card stock, slippery surfaces or dark colors no longer remain a deterrent for stamping. Decoupage is also useful with uneven surfaces, such as wicker or rough wood. As with appliqué, you can also stamp as many times as you need to in order to get the desired number of perfect images.

Begin by stamping your images onto paper or fabric; emboss if you choose to add texture. Remember that dark surfaces will show though sheer fabrics or papers, so check the density of your materials before beginning. Also, make sure to use only permanent ink, paint, or markers when coloring in your stamped images.

After the ink on your images have dried, been embossed, and fabric ink has been heat-set, cut out all of the images. Position them where desired on your project surface. If the pattern you are creating is particularly complex, lightly tape the pieces in place with a tiny piece of masking tape at one edge until you are satisfied with the placement. Generously brush one of the special decoupage pastes directly onto the project surface by gently lifting one stamped piece at a time. Apply paste to the back of each image as well, removing the masking tape and pressing each image in place as you go.

When all of the pieces have been attached, check for any missed spots where the image isn't sticking to the surface. If necessary, cut a tiny slit in the image in

Although this colorful frame appears to be difficult to do, it is deceptively simple! Four floral squares were stamped and embossed on separate white card stock, cut out, and colored in with Decorator Glazes (Plaid Enterprises). The images were then cut in half in varying proportions and angles. After placement on the colored frame was determined, each piece was attached with decoupage paste. Two additional coats of paste were applied over the images and frame to provide an even coat and extra protection.

order to get the decoupage paste underneath. Let dry completely.

Finally, cover the entire project with several light coats of paste or top sealant, letting dry between coats. A high-gloss finish will result in a faux lacquer look, whereas the satin finish has a softer, more natural appearance.

You can also apply the basic principles of the multiple layer appliqué technique to decoupage, using fabric or paper to create the multiple print images. Choose a simple large image with clearly-defined areas. Using stamping paint, stamp your image onto several differently-colored or -patterned fabrics or paper. If using fabric, attach iron-on adhesive to the back. Cut out all of the images. Leaving one image whole, cut the separate pieces out of each fabric print as desired. Iron the pieces onto the one whole image. When complete, glue the appliquéd image onto the desired surface, using the decoupage steps outlined above.

Stamping on this wood shelf presented three problems: 1) dark surface; 2) complexity of pattern; and 3) impossibility in placing the wood mount of the stamp close enough into the inside edge to stamp. Decoupage solved these problems with ease!

FRUITY POT

MATERIALS

Large outline apple and pear image rubber stamps*
Black acrylic or stamping paint
6-1/2" diameter terra cotta pot
Red, yellow, and green adhesive-backed paper (Optional: if you use non-adhesive paper, you will need a glue-stick)
Glossy decoupage paste**
Foam stamping sponge, foam plate, scissors, wide flat paintbrush

Used in this project: *#A252E Apple and #A253F Pear (Rubber Stampede) **Mod Podge (Plaid Enterprises)

1. Squeeze black acrylic or stamping paint onto a foam plate; spread it out in a 4" area. Press the apple stamp into the paint as you would an ink pad. Remove any excess paint from around the edges of the rubber. Stamp twelve apple images on the red paper and twelve on the green, reapplying paint to the stamp each time. **Clean the paint off of your stamp immediately** with a damp terry cloth rag after you have twenty-four images! (Do not submerge the stamp in water.) Repeat this step with the pear stamp, so you have a dozen each of yellow and green pear images. Let the paint dry completely.

2. Cut out all of the images from the red and yellow paper. Cut out only the leaf portions of the apple and pear from the green paper. Remove the adhesive backing from the cut-out leaves and stick them onto the apples and pears, over the corresponding leaf image areas.

Optional: If you are not using adhesive-backed paper, glue the leave sections onto the fruit image in Step 2 with glue stick. Use the decoupage paste to adhere the apples and pears onto the pot (see Step 3).

3. Beginning with pear image, remove the adhesive backing and stick it onto the pot. Continue with all of the images, fitting them together and positioning them off the edge where necessary. Trim off any excess pieces.

4. Using the paintbrush, cover the entire pot with an even layer of decoupage paste. If any portion of the images are not sticking to the pot, touch them up with paste under the edges. Add another layer of paste when dry to the touch. Let dry completely.

The rubber stamping journey doesn't have to end here—this book is just the beginning! As your rubber stamping adventures continue to unfold, the endless possibilities of this art form will take you far beyond these pages to awaken the creative spirit that lies within you!

Resources

A special thanks to the following for contributing materials and information for this book. For more information, or to find the stores nearest you carrying their products, please contact these companies directly, as listed below:

All Night Media, Inc.
P.O. Box 10607
San Rafael, CA 94912
Phone: 1-800-782-6733
www.allnightmedia.com
Wholesale only.
Manufacturer of artistic rubber stamps and distributor of accessories

Canson-Talens, Inc.
21 Industrial Drive
South Hadley, MA 01075
Phone: 1-800-628-9283
Wholesale only.
Manufacturers of photo albums and supplies

Craf-T Products, Inc.
Box 83
Fairmont, MN 56031
Phone: (507) 235-3996
Decorating Chalks and Metallic Rub-Ons

Daler-Rowney
2 Corporate Drive
Cranbury, NJ 08512-9584
Phone: (609) 655-5252
www.daler-rowney.com
Wholesale only. Imported fine art paints and supplies

DecoArt
P.O. Box 386
Stanford, KY 40484
Phone: (606) 365-3193
www.decoart.com
Wholesale only.
Manufacturer of Patio Paint (outdoor paint)

Deluxe Craft Manufacturing
1945 N. Fairfield
Chicago, IL 60647
Phone: (773) 276-6004
Outside of Illinois: 1-800-888-6004
Wholesale only.
Manufacturer of photo albums, scrapbooks, journals, and supplies

Dick Blick Art Materials
P.O. Box 1267
Galesburg, IL 61402-1267
Phone: 1-800-828-4548
www.dickblick.com
Catalog and retail distributor of art materials and books. Call or write for a free catalog (reference Dept. UR)

Duncan Enterprises
5673 E. Shields Ave.
Fresno, CA 93727
www.duncancrafts.com
Wholesale only.
Manufacturer of Aleene's Premium-Coat Acrylic paints, varnishes and mediums, and Tulip Fabric Paint

General Pencil Co.
3160 Bay Road
Redwood City, CA 94063
Phone: (650) 369-4889
Wholesale only.
Manufacturers of The Masters Brush Cleaner and Kimberly Water Color pencils

Good Stamps Stamp Goods
30901 Timberline
Willits, CA 95490
Phone: 1-800-637-6401
Wholesale and retail.
Manufacturer of artistic rubber stamps

Hero Arts Rubber Stamps, Inc.
1343 Powell Street
Emeryville, CA 94608
Phone: 1-800-822-4376
www.heroarts.com
Wholesale only.
Manufacturer and distributor of original art, handcrafted woodblock rubber stamps, and accessories

Janlynn Corporation
P.O. Box 51848
34 Front Street
Indian Orchard, MA 10051-5848
Phone: 1-800-445-5565
Email: janlnsales@aol.com
www.janlynn.com
Wholesale only.
Manufacturer of "Craftwares" pre-sewn products

The Leather Factory
P.O. Box 50429
Ft. Worth, TX 76105
Phone: 1-800-433-3201
www.leatherfactory.com
Manufacturer and distributor of leather goods and leather craft items

Maine Street Stamps
P.O. Box 14
Kingfield, ME 04947
Phone: (207) 265-2500
Email: stamps@opdag.com
www.opdag.com/ms.html
Manufacturer of artistic rubber stamps

Marks of Distinction
1030 West North Avenue, Fourth Floor
Chicago, IL 60622
Phone: (312) 335-9266
Manufacturer of artistic rubber stamps

Papercuts
246 N. Wenatchee Ave.
Wenatchee, WA 98801
Phone: 1-800-661-4399
www.papercuts.com
Distributor of paper and paper products

Plaid Enterprises, Inc.
P.O. Box 7600
Norcross, GA 30091-7600
Phone: 1-800-842-4197
www.plaidonline.com
Manufacturer of Stamp Décor, Decorator Blocks, Mod Podge, Decorator Glazes, Folk Art acrylic paints, vanishes and painting mediums

Red Hot Rubber!, Inc.
363 W. Glade
Palatine, IL 60067
Phone: (847) 991-6700
www.redhotrubber.com
Manufacturer of artistic rubber stamps

Rubber Stampede
P.O. Box 246
Berkeley, CA 94701
Phone: 1-800-632-8386
www.rstampede.com
Wholesale only.
Manufacturer of artistic rubber stamps and Decorative Foam Stamps and distributor of Decorative Stamping Paint and accessories

Savage Universal Corp.
550 E. Elliot Road
Chandler, AZ 85225
Phone: 1-800-624-8891
Wholesale only.
Manufacturer of acid-free mat mounts

Shady Lady
P.O. Box 523
Menasha, WI 54952
Phone: 1-888-722-7798
www.shades4fun.com
Manufacturer of paper lampshade kits

Stampendous, Inc.
1357 South Lewis Street
Anaheim, CA 92805-6451
Phone: 1-888-STAMPEN
www.stampendous.com
Manufacturer and distributor of artistic rubber stamps and accessories

Therm-O-Boss
Wholesale only.
Manufacturer of embossing powders.
www.thermoboss.com

Therm O Web, Inc.
770 Glenn Avenue
Wheeling, IL 60090
Phone: 1-800-323-0799
Email:
cpdsales@thermoweb.com
www.thermoweb.com
Wholesale only.
Manufacturer of iron-on (HeatnBond) and pressure sensitive PeelnStick and Keep a Memory adhesives and laminates for fabric and memory making.

Tombow
2000 Newpoint Place Parkway
Suite 500
Lawrenceville, GA 30043
Phone: 1-800-835-3232
www.tombowusa.com
Wholesale only.
Manufacturer of Dual Brush-Pen Markers, Mono Adhesive and Liquid Glue

Tsukineko, Inc.
15411 NE 95th Street
Redmond, WA 98052
Phone: 1-800-769-6633
Fax: (425) 883-7418
www.tsukineko.com
Wholesale only.
Manufacturer of Encore! Ultimate Metallic Pigment Ink, Fabrico Premium Multi-Purpose Craft Ink and Dual Markers, Emboss Dual Pen and Embossing Stamp Pad, Kaleidacolor, and Impress Dye Inkpads

Walnut Hollow Farm
1409 State Road 23
Dodgeville, WI 53533
Phone: 1-800-950-5101
Manufacturer of unfinished wood products

Wrights
P.O. Box 398
85 South Street
West Warren, MA 01092
Phone: (877) 5WRIGHT
Email: help@wrights.com
www.wrights.com
Wholesale only.
Manufacturer of trims, ribbons, and lace

Credits for Images Used in Photos

All of the following images were used with permission.

Page 13 (note cards and bookmark) (top left) #C457 Beach Grass (Hero Arts Rubber Stamps, Inc.); #G4041 Poppies, #F3030 Singing Kitty (Maine Street Stamps); #PR-8 Dancing Girl (Marks of Distinction); (top right) #A121 Ribbon Posies,
#J043 Bold Butterfly (Stampendous, Inc.); (bot. left) #F4059 Looking Glass Fairy (Maine Street Stamps); #1174 Full Bloom Rose (Hero Arts Rubber Stamps, Inc.); (bot. right) #G1045 Country Angel (Hero Arts Rubber Stamps, Inc.); #G034 Birthday Whimsy (Stampendous, Inc.)

Page 14 (gift box and
card) #A037 Crayon, #C235 Paintbrush (Red Hot Rubber!, Inc.)

Pages 15-16 (photo steps) #G1045 Country Angel (Hero Arts Rubber Stamps, Inc.)

Page 16 (note cards with repeated patterns) #A037 Crayon, #C235 Paintbrush (Red Hot Rubber!, Inc.)

Page 17 (four different note cards with random repeat) From left to right: #A037 Crayon (Red Hot Rubber!, Inc.); #BO-195 9 Hearts/Stems Flowers Border (Marks of Distinction); #0270D Spiral Sun (All Night Media, Inc.); #F31 Ink Splats Texture (Stampendous, Inc.);

Page 19 (masked rabbit and eggs) #363D Big Bunny (All Night Media, Inc.); #C1149 Primrose Egg, #D1148 Daisy Egg (Maine Street Stamps)

Page 20 (Happy Holidays note card) #A1321C Country Star Patch, #A1422C Christmas Stocking Patch (Rubber Stampede); #F125 Happy Holidays (Hero Arts Rubber Stamps, Inc.)

Page 20 (wrapping paper and card with pattern stamped off the edge) #F253 Serene Sun, #F204 Big Sunflower (Hero Arts Rubber Stamps, Inc.); #N30 Peacock Feather (Stampendous, Inc.)

Page 22 (Happy birthday cards and corresponding stamps) #D309 Happy Birthday, #D303 Ice Cream Cone (Red Hot Rubber!, Inc.), #489D Fish Lips, #546E Tiny, #547F Max (All Night Media, Inc.); #D309 Happy

Birthday (Red Hot Rubber!, Inc.), #F447 Patterned Happy Birthday (Hero Arts Rubber Stamps, Inc.)

Page 24 (purple and teal note card) #271A Diamond, #319D Royal Star (all Night Media, Inc.)

Page 24 (flower note card) #503D Flower Power (All Night Media, Inc.)

Page 24 (tea note card) #B094 Tea Postage Stamp (Hero Arts Rubber Stamps, Inc.)

Page 25 (horizontal girl card) #G4522 In the Meadow (Maine Street Stamps)

Page 25 (vertical girl card) #G-4520 Daisies For You (Maine Street Stamps)

Page 25 (Happy Birthday note card) #D039 Happy Birthday (Red Hot Rubber!, Inc.); #G-3133 Wave Border (Maine Street Stamps)

Page 26 (rose note card) #91-83E Rose in Bloom (Good Stamps Stamp Goods)

Page 26 (horse and sunflower note card) #F204 Big Sunflower (Hero Arts Rubber Stamps, Inc.); #186H Running Horses (All Night Media, Inc.)

Page 26 (sunflower and "Your kindness…" note card) #F204 Big Sunflower (Hero Arts Rubber Stamps, Inc.); #E113 Your Kindness (Stampendous, Inc.)

Page 26 (baby with stars

Page 63 (child's birthday party ensemble) #023 You're Invited, #R0002 Balloon Frame, #G034 Birthday Whimsy (Stampendous, Inc.); #C249 Large Cupcake (Red Hot Rubber!, Inc.); #218 Cat Balloon, #286G Scribble Thank You (All Night Media, Inc.)

Page 63 (gift boxes and bags) (top left) #F539 Border Collie Pup, Bone #A101(Red Hot Rubber!, Inc.); (top right) #A1440G Christmas Wish (Rubber Stampede); (bot.) #A252E Apple, #A1768C Love & Kisses (Rubber Stampede)

Page 63 (cat gift box) #546E Tiny, #766D Meow Border, #2952Q Jive Alphabet (All Night Media, Inc.)

Page 64 (several types of projects, including album covers, pages, and frames) (top) #A1249E Scallop Shell (Rubber Stampede); #G-3133 Wave Border (Maine Street Stamps); (bot. left) #ID-12 Paint Tube Frame (Marks of Distinction); (center) #C-4048 Eyelet Butterfly (Maine Street Stamps); (right) #Z830G Cowhide Frame (Rubber Stampede)

Page 65 (child coming out of a gift box) #AA024 Single Note, #S-JG Gift Box Set (Stampendous, Inc.)

Page 65 (autumn leaves back-to-school page) #E488 Large Fall Leaf (Hero Arts Rubber Stamps, Inc.)

Page 66 (photos cut in heart shapes and photo collage) #A909E Hearts Abound (Rubber Stampede); #901F Swirl I Love You (All Night

Media, Inc.); #2952-Q Jive Alphabet (All Night Media, Inc.)

Page 67 (checkered frame) #A1856G Lace Frame (Rubber Stampede)

Page 67 (stars page) #LL404 Country Border (Hero Arts Rubber Stamps)

Page 67 (layered paper page) #F31 Ink Splats Texture (Stampendous, Inc.)

Page 68 (winter scene frame) #F611 Snowy Trees, #A212 Solitary Snowflake (Hero Arts Rubber Stamps, Inc.)

Page 68 (baby bottle page) #C206 Baby Bottle (Red Hot Rubber!, Inc.); #G-1162 Pat-A-Cake (Maine Street Stamps)

Page 68 (watermelon page) #B046 Watermelon (Stampendous, Inc.)

Page 68 ("crystal ball" page) #297J Crystal Globe (All Night Media Inc.)

Page 70 (mountain scene corners page) #F-937 Triangle Corner 2 (Maine Street Stamps)

Page 70 (bride with rose corners page) #A802F Romantic Rose Corner (Rubber Stampede)

Page 70 (hammock with marble-textured corners page) #F40 Marbled Clover Texture (Stampendous, Inc.)

Page 71 (girls with heart and quilt corners page) #QN013 Quilt Frame, #SSM09 Country Buttons Mini Stamp Set (Stampendous, Inc.)

Page 71 (farm scene with cut-up frame page) #QN013 Quilt Frame (Stampendous, Inc.)

Page 71 (dog pages and little boy frame) #148B Baseball, #306C Dog Bones (All Night Media, Inc.)

Page 72 (ski page) #642F Snowman, #465G Fir Tree, #665D Snowflake (All Night Media, Inc.)

Page 72 (princess pages) #N036 Flowered Banner (Stampendous, Inc.); #A009 Crown, #J906 Gumball Girl (Red Hot Rubber!, Inc.); #448C Crown, #409K Antique Oval Frame (All Night Media, Inc.); #TB-130 Castle, #TB-142 Large Crown, #TB-40 Crown (Marks of Distinction)

Page 74 (panda album cover) #K956 Panda Hugs (Red Hot Rubber!, Inc.); #A-4404 Tile (Maine Street Stamps); #2952Q Jive Alphabet Set (All Night Media, Inc.); #63003 Primitive Set-Decorative Stamping (Rubber Stampede)

Page 74 (flower album cover) #BO-176 Large Shaded Flower Corner (Marks of Distinction)

Page 76 (box with swirls and round box with photos in frames) #A1856G Lace Frame, #63003 Primitive Set (Rubber Stampede); #QN026 Funky Frame (Stampendous, Inc.); #ID-12 Paint Tube Frame (Marks of Distinction)

Page 77 (shoe project and castle memory album) #B-4401 Stencil Triangle, #C-4418 Spectator Pump, #C-4417 40's Shoe 1, #C-4419

40's Shoe 2, #H-4426 Frame (Maine Street Stamps); #A952E Swirls (Rubber Stampede); #A-4400 Stencil Tile (Maine Street Stamps); #TB142 Large Crown, #TB40 Crown, #TB130 Castle (Marks of Distinction); #448C Crown (All Night Media, Inc.); #A009 Crown (Red Hot Rubber!, Inc.)

Page 77 (cat in rose frame) #A1562G Romantic Rose Frame (Rubber Stampede)

Page 79 (unusual embossing powder colors on strip) #231C Swirl Rose (All Night Media)

Page 79 (pearls over ink colors) #A1657F Dream Garden Rose Vase (Rubber Stampede)

Page 82 (faux finish verdigris and enamelware bookmark) #319D Royal Star, #271A Diamond (All Night Media, Inc.); #320B Small Spiral (All Night Media, Inc.)

Page 82 (swirl recipe box) #310F Large Swirl, #320B Small Swirl (All Night Media, Inc.)

Page 82 (egg frame and cactus card) D-1148 Daisy Egg, #C-1145 Lace Egg 1, #C-1146 Lace Egg 2, #C1149 Primrose (Maine Street Stamps); #C352 Big Thank You (Hero Arts Rubber Stamps, Inc.), #L027 Small Saguaro (Stampendous, Inc.)

Page 82 (funky flower folder) #503D Flower Power (All Night Media, Inc.)

Page 84 (fuzzy flocking and puffy powders) #58-23E Solo Pansy (Good

Stamps Stamp Goods)
Page 84 (foiled bow)
#C072 Striped Bow
(Stampendous, Inc.)

Page 85 (four different
effects on sun swirl)
#270D Spiral Sun (All
Night Media, Inc.)

Page 85 (sea horse pres-
sure-embossed in gold
and copper foil) #CS-3
Seahorse (Marks of
Distinction)

Page 86 (tea cup invita-
tion) #Q006 China Tea
Cup (Stampendous, Inc.)

Page 86 (oval rose box)
#A1248E Stained Glass
Rose Oval (Rubber
Stampede)

Page 89 (3-D projects:
sunflower box, fish
picture, "Katie" door
hanger) (top left) #490D
Tropical Fish, #4503-4
Under Seas Adventures Set
(All Night Media, Inc.);
(bot. left) #A1102E
Monkey Fern (Rubber
Stampede), Katie (All
Night Media, Inc.); (top
right) #F204 Big
Sunflower (Hero Arts
Rubber Stamps)

Page 89 (butterfly picture)
#345E Butterfly, #476F
Tulips (All Night Media,
Inc.)

Page 97 (winter diorama)
#G1266 Winter Cottage,
#C1308 Fir Tree (Maine
Street Stamps); #H110
Whitetail Deer
(Stampendous, Inc.);
#F611 Snowy Trees (Hero
Arts Rubber stamps);
#611C Snowflake Cluster
(All Night Media, Inc.)

Page 97 (butterfly on a
sunflower in a vase)
#G1243 Large Butterfly,
#A1592E Garden Urn
(Rubber Stampede);

#F204 Big Sunflower
(Hero Arts Rubber
Stamps, Inc.)

Page 99 (dog/pencil
Happy Birthday note
card) #C247 Scamp (Red
Hot Rubber!, Inc.); #ID-
15 Fat Pencil (Marks of
Distinction); #14-24B
Scissors (Good Stamps
Stamp Goods); #AA017
Tiny Paw, #G034 Birthday
Whimsy (Stampendous,
Inc.). Also used: Tombow
Dual Brush-Pen Markers #
025, 623, 821, 912, 990,
991, N15, N79, and N89)

Page 99 (snowman and
mouse/cheese note cards)
#B1201 Star (Maine Street
Stamps); #G018 Sand/
Snow (Stampendous,
Inc.); #642F Snowman
(All Night Media, Inc.);
#A049 Colby the Mouse,
#D348 Swiss Cheese (Red
Hot Rubber!, Inc.)

Page 100 (gift bag, torn
tissue hearts, garden jour-
nal album) (top left)
#B1306 Maple Leaf, #F
1307 Bare Branches
(Maine Street Stamps);
(top right) #A952E Swirls
(Rubber Stampede);
MK73 Man & Woman
Conversing (Marks of
Distinction); #2952Q Jive
Alphabet Set (All Night
Media, Inc.); (bot.) #231C
Swirl Rose (All Night
Media, Inc.); #N048
Birdhouse Fence
(Stampendous, Inc.);
#A1591E Watering Can
(Rubber Stampede)

Page 100 (collage box)
#2902-Q Ornamental
Stamp Squares Set,
Ornamental Alphabet (All
Night Media, Inc.)

Page 101 (Projects using
wiggle eyes, confetti,
ribbons, etc.) (top left)
#F253 Serene Sun (Hero
Arts Rubber Stamps, Inc.);

(bot. left) #G034 Birthday
Whimsy (Stampendous,
Inc.), #532B Happy Face
(All Night Media, Inc.);
(top right) #G221 Letters
(Maine Street Stamps),
#A909E Hearts Abound
(Rubber Stampede); (bot.
right) #F253 Serene Sun
(Hero Arts Rubber
Stamps, Inc.), #F1731
Rainbow Colors (Maine
Street Stamps)

Page 103 (garden gloves)
#503D Flower Power (All
Night Media, Inc.)

Page 104 (bibs) #C206
Baby Bottle, #D332 Rattle
(Red Hot Rubber!, Inc.);
#TB-116 Footprints
(Marks of Distinction)

Page 104 (iris bag)
#A1243F Stained Glass Iris
(Rubber Stampede)

Page 110 (fabric pear)
#A253F Pear (Rubber
Stampede)

Page 110 (pansy doily
pillow) #R032 Pansy Patch
(Stampendous, Inc.)

Page 113 (leather belt)
#A854E Jaguar Print
(Rubber Stampede)

Page 113 (leather coast-
ers) 2908Q Doodles Set
(All Night Media)

Page 113 (leather
barrette) #700.21 The
Flower Tray Collection
(Rubber Stampede)

Page 116 (rose frame,
lamp, and wall) #64006
Spring Garden Set, #6023
Decorative Scroll, #202893
Whimsical Rose from the
Decorative Stamping
series and #A1563G
Romantic Roses Large
Bouquet, #A1566E
Romantic Roses Small
Bouquet, #A805B
Romantic Rose (Rubber

Stampede); Lamp shade
kit (Shady Lady);
Unfinished wood rectan-
gular frame and 7" lamp
base (Walnut Hollow)

Page 119 (hand holding
spacing strip next to first
rose imprint) #202893
Whimsical Rose
Decorative Stamp (Rubber
Stampede)

Page 119 (angle strip
triangle held next to
images already stamped)
#64001 Decorative
Stamping Country Folk
Art set (Rubber
Stampede)

Page 119 (tulip table)
#53213 Tulips Decorator
Blocks (Plaid Enterprises).
Table primed with
Aleene's Premium-Coat
Acrylic paint (#OC153
Dusty Blue) and Deco Art
Gel Stain (#DS25
Bleached Pine White).
Images stamped with
Decorator Glazes (Plaid
Enterprises) in the follow-
ing colors: Burgundy,
Banana, Cerulean, Hot
Magenta, Mango, Paprika,
New Pine, and Sage
Green.

Page 120 (mini bird-
houses) #AA048 Violet
(Stampendous, Inc.);
#A1221 Quilted Flower
(Hero Arts Rubber
Stamps, Inc.); #372G Ivy
Border, #100D Three
Little Vases (All Night
Media, Inc.)

Page 120 (wooden bear
shelf) 9" Mini Unfinished
Wood Shelf #8844 by
Walnut Hollow; #H084
Large Antique Bears (Hero
Arts Rubber Stamps, Inc.);
#A-922 Flake (Maine
Street Stamps)

Page 120 (wood chip box)
#A-4405 (Maine Street
Stamps)

Page 121 (three different versions of the clock) #0635G Winter Trees (All Night Media, Inc.)

Page 121 (wooden frame with vegetable picture) #B-1119 Carrot, #F-1127 Cabbage, #F128 Tomato, #1131 Onions (Maine Street Stamps)

Page 121 (Detailed insert and kitchen cabinet) Decorative Stamping #61010 Checkerboard Border and #63001 Vegetable Set (Rubber Stampede)

Page 122 (child's picnic table) Decorative Stamping #64007 Alphabet Set and #61004 Five Point Star (Rubber Stampede); Patio Paint (DecoArt): Summer Sky Blue (DCP10), Sunshine Yellow (DCP06), Geranium Red (DCP07), and Wrought Iron Black (DCP21)

Page 122 (mailbox) Decorative Stamping #64006 Spring Garden Set (Rubber Stampede); Patio Paint((DecoArt) as follows: Box base-coated in: Foxglove Pink (DCP02), Light Eucalyptus Green (DCP23), and Cloud White (DCP14). Images stamped in: Pine Green (DCP04) and Patio Brick (DCP16)

Page 122 (planter box) Decorative Stamping #64001 Country Folk Art Set (Rubber Stampede); #21210 Unfinished 10" wood window box (Walnut Hollow)

Page 125 (snowman mistake) #A1440G Christmas Wish (Rubber Stampede)

Page 126 (star mistake) #H1147 Big Solid Star (Hero Arts Rubber Stamps, Inc.)

Page 126 (cat mistake) #OR-77 Cookie & Sarah Jane (Marks of Distinction)

Page 126 (swirl mistake) #63003 Primitive Set (Rubber Stampede)

Page 126 (Happy Birthday note card) #D309 Happy Birthday (Red Hot Rubber!, Inc.); #91-83E Rose in Bloom (Good Stamps Stamp Goods)

Page 127 (floral border note card) #E-1218 Deco Floral Border (Maine Street Stamps)

Page 127 (invitation mistake and "colored") #H023 You're Invited (Stampendous, Inc.)

Page 127 (rose mistake and colored) #1216 Rose (Marks of Distinction)

Page 128 (cut-out cats and note card) #A742 Monarch Butterfly (Hero Arts Rubber Stamps, Inc.); #452E Clouds, #476F Tulips, #344E Flutter of Butterflies (All Night Media, Inc.); #OR-77 Cookie & Sarah Jane (Marks of Distinction)

Page 130 (aquatic scene vest) #A1249E Scallop Shell, #A1251E Nautilus Shell (Rubber Stampede); #D349 Large Grouper Fish (Hero Arts Rubber Stamps, Inc.); #F622 Tropical Fish (Red Hot Rubber!, Inc.); #O488E Angelfish (All Night Media, Inc.)

Page 132 (Pumpkin wall hanging) #G601 Jack-O-Lantern (Red Hot Rubber!, Inc.)

Page 134 (star shelf) #H1147 Big Solid Star (Hero Arts Rubber Stamps, Inc.)

Page 134 (floral patch frame) #3765 Magnolia (All Night Media, Inc.)

Glossary

Appliqué: A crafting technique that involves attaching fabric shapes or images onto another fabric surface.

Archival quality: Types of paper, ink, and other supplies that will not damage photos. Non-reactive archival supplies are all acid-free; archival papers are both acid- and lignan-free.

Back-print: Unwanted ink transferred onto a stamping surface resulting from ink accidentally clinging to a non-image portion of the stamp.

Bilateral image: An image where, if a line were drawn down the center, each half would be a mirror image of the other.

Brayering: A coloring process in which a tool, called a brayer, picks up ink or paint on its roller and is then rolled over a stamping surface to transfer the pigment onto it.

Collage: Multi-layer art form centered around a theme that uses widely varying materials and three-dimensional objects.

Complementary colors: The basic color wheel contains the three **primary** colors (red, yellow, blue) and the three **secondary** colors (orange, green, purple) that appear when two primary colors are mixed together. **Complementary** colors are those colors that appear opposite each other on the color wheel. Each of these complementary pairs are made up of one primary color and the secondary color that is a mixture of the remaining two primary colors.

Container image: Outline stamp images with large blank inside areas. They are especially suitable to use in mortise masking.

Decoupage: A crafting technique involving cutting and gluing flat paper shapes, pictures, drawings, stamped images, etc. onto another surface.

Dye ink: Quick-drying water-based ink suitable for use on both non-glossy and glossy paper.

Embellishment supplies: Tools or materials used to enhance a rubber-stamped project.

Embossing (technical name, **Thermography**): A technique in which embossing powder is sprinkled over an image that has been stamped with a slow-drying pigment ink and then carefully heated until the powder melts to form a hard, raised image.

Embossing ink: Clear or lightly-tinted pigment ink

used with opaque embossing powders.

Fabric or Textile ink: Pigment or solvent-based ink used on surfaces such as fabric or leather where extra permanence is required.

Faux finish: The duplication of textures and colors found on natural surfaces, such as wood or granite, using man-made products and special painting techniques.

Foam cushion: The portion of a stamp that is sandwiched between the rubber die and wood mount.

Heat setting: A process of applying heat to images that have been stamped with pigment-based fabric or textile inks that require this step to give them permanence, especially when exposed to water. Heat setting is most often done using a non-steam set iron. The time and temperature vary, depending on the surface that is being heat-set.

Incomplete imprint: Refers to a stamped image that has not come out clearly or completely.

Masking: A technique that involves temporarily covering up a stamped image with a duplicate cut-out image and then stamping the same or different image, partially overlap-

ping the first image, to create the illusion of overlap.

Mortise masking: A technique in which the outside area of a stamped container image is temporarily covered, and other stamp images are then stamped on the inside area of the container image.

Mount: The wood, polymer, or foam handle of a stamp.

Outline image rubber or foam stamp: A stamp whose image area contains a line drawing with unfilled areas that can be colored in after the image has been stamped.

Over-coat: Describes when too much paint has been applied to the image area of a stamp.

Over-stamp: To stamp images on top of other images that have already been stamped on a surface.

Pigment ink: Slow-drying colored ink primarily used with clear or opaque embossing powder. It can also be used on surfaces other than paper.

Repeat design: Stamping one or more images over and over with or without a specific pattern.

Resist: A property contained in certain materials that can repel water or liquid-based substances.

Rubber die: The portion of a rubber stamp that contains the trimmed rubber image.

Score: Usually done with an X-acto knife, a line is cut that does not completely go through the material it is cut on. This process enables card stock and other paper surfaces to be crisply folded or bent.

Sponging: A coloring technique using a small stamping sponge and ink. The stamping sponge is first pounced onto the ink pad or colored on with a marker. The pigment that has been transferred to the sponge is then applied to the stamping surface with short dabbing motions.

Solid image rubber or foam stamp: A stamp whose image area is completely filled with pigment when stamped.

Symmetrical/ Asymmetrical design: Design that appears equally balanced with the same colors, sizes, shapes, etc. (symmetrical) or unequally balanced with differing colors, sizes, shapes, etc. (asymmetrical).

Index